M000164114

gift of faith, care deeply for the Church of England. Adrian draws his inspiration initially from apparently superficial incidents and details, but as he gets drawn in he plumbs the depths and writes most movingly about the spiritual life and the problems of pursuing it in a largely indifferent and often hostile world. He claims his reflections are merely random meditations, but in fact they display the workings of a profound and mature intelligence.

ROGER LOCKYER
Reader Emeritus in History in the University of London

NEBUCHADNEZZAR'S MARMALADE POT

& OTHER REFLECTIONS

ADRIAN LEAK

The Book Guild Ltd

First published in Great Britain in 2017 by
The Book Guild Ltd
9 Priory Business Park
Wistow Road, Kibworth
Leicestershire, LE8 0RX
Freephone: 0800 999 2982
www.bookguild.co.uk
Email: info@bookguild.co.uk
Twitter: @bookguild

Typeset in Aldine401 BT

Printed and bound in Great Britain by CPI Group (UK) Ltd, Croydon, CR0 4YY

ISBN 978 1912083 947

British Library Cataloguing in Publication Data.
A catalogue record for this book is available from the British Library.

To
Josephine
with love

CONTENTS

PREFACE

Dear Reader,

Many of the reflections which make up this volume originated as 'Letters from the Rectory', published in the parish magazine of St Michael and All Angels, Withyham with All Saints, Blackham in East Sussex. I am therefore grateful to the magazine editor, Richard Pardey, for his permission to reproduce them in this format. I apologise to any long-suffering parishioners who may remember having read them before.

Some of these brief passages are shaped by the sequence of the Church's Calendar and the topics are linked to the great Christian festivals of Christmas, Epiphany, Easter, Ascension and Pentecost. The others are less specific, arising from the daily contingencies of a country parish – what the Book of Common Prayer calls, 'the changes and chances of this mortal life'.

If there is a common thread – and none was intended – it may be seen in the reflection placed at the beginning of this collection, and from which it takes its name, *Nebuchadnezzar's Marmalade Pot:*

'It is the ordinary that gathers us into the commonwealth of the human race: a commonwealth which transcends barriers of race and creed, time and place. It is the commonplace, the shared material of life, which Jesus consecrated in the bread and wine, and which he transfigured when in his risen glory he invited those tired fishermen, who had toiled all night, to join him for breakfast on the shore of Galilee'.

In offering these reflections, I ask your indulgence and

hope that you will enjoy them for what they are: the random thoughts of an imperfect parish priest.

Adrian Leak
Bramley
Surrey

NEBUCHADNEZZAR'S MARMALADE POT

Colonel Henry Rawlinson was a celebrated traveller and amateur archaeologist in the nineteenth century. He returned from one of his expeditions in Mesopotamia with a rare treasure. He had dug it up, he said, in the ruins of King Nebuchadnezzar's palace. It was a small sealed jar containing what had once been marmalade.

He presented it to the young Queen Victoria. Although her journal is silent on the subject, it would be pleasing to think that Nebuchadnezzar's marmalade pot graced the breakfast table at Windsor. Perhaps – who knows?– the queen, as she gazed across the table at her beloved Albert, might have reflected with relief upon the happy contrast between the rise of the House of Saxe-Coburg, with its golden promise, and the fall of the House of Babylon, with all its concomitant ghastliness.

Archaeologists do us a great service. They remind us that what endures in the story of mankind is the commonplace. Broken cooking vessels, discarded sandals, old laundry lists and marmalade pots recall us to a proper sense of proportion. They teach us to suspect any view of history which is out of scale with the breakfast table.

There is in Sunderland a church whose Saxon porch is as it was when Bede worshipped there as a boy. He was seven when he joined the monastery at Monkwearmouth – the same age as some of the children who today visit the Saxon site on school visits. Like them, he must have wondered at the interlaced serpents carved upon the entrance. Like them, he must have instinctively put out his hand to touch those mysterious figures of Saxon art – what boy wouldn't? Like them, no doubt, he was told, too late, 'Don't touch!'

Before time erodes completely those ancient carvings, or conservationists prudently put them beyond reach, how many young hands must have felt those stones and, at one degree of separation, touched each other, across the centuries, joined in a shared involuntary gesture – and one of those hands was Bede's.

History is witness to our shared ordinariness. It is the ordinary that gathers us into the commonwealth of the human race: a commonwealth which transcends barriers of race and creed, time and place. It is the commonplace, the shared material of life, which Jesus consecrated in the bread and wine, and which he transfigured when in his risen glory he invited those tired fishermen, who had toiled all night, to join him for breakfast on the shore of Galilee.

'Though we are many, we are one body, because we all share in one bread', we proclaim at the Eucharist. And what a sharing it is, such as our poor imaginations can only begin to grasp.

BONFIRE NIGHT

You know how it is on bonfire night: grown-ups and children gather in a field, booted and muffled against the November chill, as they excitedly watch the flames take hold, the branches crackling and spitting, and sparks flying into the sky. It is a wonderful sight, that great towering inferno.

But take a moment to turn your eyes away from the fire. Look now at the faces around you. And there you will see a sight more wonderful still: those faces caught in the light of the flames – transformed, enhanced against the surrounding dark each face with its own unique and dazzling beauty, edged in flame against the night.

Soon, just a few weeks after Bonfire Night, will come Advent with a different fire. Malachi, 'the messenger' of ancient Judah, warned of the coming day 'that would burn as an oven when all the arrogant will be stubble; the day that comes shall burn them up'.

Five centuries later the Christian church saw a link between Malachi and John the Baptist, the terrifying forerunner of the Messiah. 'Christ will baptise you with the Holy Spirit and with fire', said John. 'His winnowing-fork is in his hand, and he will clear his threshing-floor and will gather his wheat into his granary, but the chaff he will burn with unquenchable fire.'

The image of Christ threshing our souls is not one on which artists often dwell. We avert our eyes. We prefer to turn our faces away from the flames of Christ's cauterising love.

But, then, how would we have God treat us? As an indulgent father always ready to overlook our faults? Or worse, a distant sovereign in whose eyes our petty misdemeanours are of little consequence, and to whom we do not really matter? That is a chilling thought.

In the Biblical view it is divine judgement that rescues us from insignificance. We *do* matter. Our actions, our words, our thoughts *do* count. The bad ones and the good ones. They count because we are infinitely precious in the eyes of God. He takes us seriously enough to judge us. But like Jacob we resist his embrace and are wounded by his love.

> *Who then devised the torment? Love.*
> *Love is the unfamiliar Name*
> *Behind the hands that wove*
> *The intolerable shirt of flame*
> *Which human power cannot remove.*
> *We only live, only suspire*
> *Consumed by either fire or fire.*
>
> (T S Eliot, *Little Gidding*)

Those faces turned tonight towards the flames and transfigured briefly against the surrounding dark, how will they endure the coming years? Not without pain, that's for sure.

But also with joy, as they are drawn closer to the source of that dazzling light and come to know, each in their own way, the power of his healing love.

PRAYING FOR THE SOULS OF THE DEPARTED

Remember, remember the fifth of November: gunpowder, treason and plot.

The old rhyme recalls Guy Fawkes and his conspiracy to blow up Parliament. Because he failed, we can now treat the whole thing as a joke. The horror of that intended act of terrorism has faded. What has *not* faded from the mind is the horror of the two World Wars. We have all that footage of old newsreels to keep reminding us.

Remembrance Sunday strikes in the mind a greater resonance as each year passes. It has become an occasion for us all, of whatever age or nationality, to recall the victims of war.

November is also the month when we pray for the souls of the departed. All Souls day falls on the 2nd, following All Saints on the 1st. The Church of England used to be reluctant to pray for the souls of those who had died. It was felt to be either unnecessary (if they were in heaven then what need could they have of our prayers?) or heretical (if they were *not* in heaven then did we really think that we could manipulate God by our pleading – and if we could, then what sort of God would he be?)

But praying for our families and friends is not done to win favours. It is done because it is the natural thing to do – to speak their names in our hearts as we place ourselves in the presence of God. It is a sort of holding hands or hugging each other within the greater embrace of God. And if we do this when they are still with us in this life, why stop when they have gone into the next?

John Donne, the seventeenth century poet and Dean of St Paul's, wrote some words which were later refashioned as a prayer:

Bring us, O Lord God, at our last awakening into the house and gate of heaven, to enter into that gate and dwell in that house, where there shall be no darkness nor dazzling but one equal light, no noise nor silence but one equal music, no fears nor hopes but one equal possession, no ends nor beginnings but one equal eternity, in the habitations of thy majesty and glory, world without end. Amen.

We shall not be alone as we go through that gate, and what wonderful company we have been promised in the rooms of our Father's house.

REMEMBRANCE SUNDAY

One of the most shocking things about war is that its victims are often so young. Those who are killed in battle and those who are severely injured are mostly in their twenties, sometimes their teens.

In the churchyard at Worplesdon, near Guildford, there is a headstone which tells that a young lad called H J Deakin, who served in the Royal Navy on HMS Powerful died at sea on 19th September 1918. His age was seventeen. His rank was 'Boy 2nd Class J92245'. It is a poignant statement, and it is sad that the boy is recalled only by surname, initials, rank and number. That small and important personal detail – his Christian name – is missing.

And that is the second shocking thing about war. It depersonalises. It reduces its victims to surname, rank and number.

When we send into battle young men and women to fight on our behalf, we are putting them into situations where they have to be ready to kill or be killed. For our safety they are trained to inflict death: to pump a burst of automatic fire at a sniper visible in an upstairs window; to pull the pin and lob a grenade into a room where the suspected enemy is hiding; to press the button that fires the missile that destroys the enemy's HQ and blows a dozen men and women to pieces.

To do such things on our behalf and for the greater safety of the world, we are asking them to suspend, to switch off, all that part of themselves which is most truly human. We are asking them to blot out from their minds the knowledge that the sniper in the upstairs window, the enemy hiding in the deserted building, the dozen personnel in the targeted HQ are people like them, with families and homes, parents and children, favourite pop groups, preferred football teams, and all the hopes and dreams of youth.

As combatants they must depersonalise the enemy in their sights, else they could never pull the trigger. War brutalises us all. It must. The miracle is that when it is over, the participants (most, not all) are able to recover their humanity. Hostilities cease, the soldiers are demobilised, the bridges rebuilt, the barbed wire removed. And then, years later, the veterans return to the old battlefields to remember their comrades who never came home and to swap stories about a distant and receding past.

At the service on Remembrance Sunday the names of those killed in the two World Wars are read out. We do this for them every year. By naming them we are restoring to them their humanity, their identity as individuals – people who were once the children of this parish. We are calling to mind that they are not mere statistics, known to history only by surname, rank and number. They are each a unique person, precious in the sight of God.

Remembering the fallen by name – even when the name is all we know – is our way of reminding ourselves and the world that each of these young people is counted and loved and highly valued in the eyes of our heavenly Father.

MRS BOEHM'S PARTY

Mrs Edmund Boehm, the society hostess, achieved the peak of success when on Wednesday June 21st, 1815, the Prince Regent attended a dance at her residence in St James's Square. The evening, however, was disturbed by the kind of incident a hostess dreads. Just as the guests were taking their partners for the first quadrille, a wild-eyed figure in bloodstained uniform burst in. It was Major the Honourable Henry Percy. He carried the Duke of Wellington's Waterloo despatch announcing the defeat of Napoleon.

You can imagine the stir – the buzz – the commotion: wheezing old veterans of the Peninsular campaign calling for brandy; young men shouting 'Huzzah'; demure maidens crying 'La' behind their fans; and stout matrons quite fainting away with the excitement of it all (the rooms too hot; the food too rich; the stays too tight). And, as if that was not bad enough, the Prince, never one to miss the opportunity of *le grand geste*, insisted on going out on to the balcony and addressing his subjects in the square below.

Mrs Boehm was appalled as she witnessed her carefully planned evening unravel before her eyes. She declared later that she 'was much annoyed with the Battle of Waterloo' as it had spoilt her party.

History is full of unwelcome interruptions; some real and disastrous, like the writing on the wall at Belshazzar's Feast, foretelling the fall of the royal house of Babylon; some imagined and disappointing, like Saki's account of the Archangel's attempt to sound the Last Trump only to be told that he had clashed with the last day of Henley; and some tantalising, like the one inflicted upon the poet Coleridge by the unexpected visitor from Porlock, leaving us only the unfinished, haunting fragment of *Kubla Khan*.

There is a view which holds that there is no interruption which does not find its resolution in the longer perspective. What at close range looks like a crashing incongruity, when viewed at a greater distance fits neatly into place. Upon further reflection Mrs Boehm might well have considered that her evening was indeed a most fitting conclusion to a train of events which had begun six days before in Brussels at the Duchess of Richmond's Ball. And had she so reflected she would have drawn much comfort from this juxtaposition and symmetry.

For Christians, the greatest interruption of the course of history is the Birth of Christ. It was unexpected: without the angel's salutation who could expect such a birth? It was unnatural: well, who *was* the father? Incongruous: why would God choose to be born in such obscurity? It was unwise: could universal redemption really be entrusted to such a fragile agency? And yet to the eye of faith the interruption is no accident, but the key to all that has happened in history before and since, and all that will hereafter. It is the standard by which our ideas of power and status are judged. By that birth not only mankind, but nature herself has been re-ordered in a new creation.

And that is why we wish each other a 'Happy Christmas'.

CHRISTMAS: PLUM PUDDING & TWELFTH CAKE

On Christmas Day, 1660, Samuel Pepys went to church in the morning, had dinner at home with his wife and brother, went to church again in the afternoon, fell asleep during the sermon, passed the evening in reading and playing his lute, before retiring at midnight to bed. He was 26 years old. He was not a dull dog, and we can be certain that if his fellow Londoners had been partying, he would have been there carousing with the best of them. Why then did he make so little of the festival? Well, Pepys was a city man, and most Christmas customs were rural.

Few of them have much to do with religion. Like our forebears, we go to church to celebrate the birth of Christ, and then we give ourselves over to celebrations which are frankly pagan in origin. It was ever thus. Why should we complain? Of these, the Christmas Dinner is the most enduring. In earlier centuries, because of rural poverty, many country people depended upon the hospitality of the 'big house' or the parsonage.

The Reverend Samuel Woodforde (father of the diarist) was Rector of Ansford in Somerset from 1719 to 1771. He and his family were regularly joined for their Christmas dinner by fifteen 'poor and old' parishioners. They were good trenchermen. On Christmas Day, 1764, they consumed a thirty pound rump of beef and three large plum puddings. The parish clerk carved the meat.

Another tradition we all enjoy is the Christmas cake. Originally it was part of the Twelfth Night celebrations, and was called the Twelfth Cake. Country people would bake their twelfth cakes with a hole in the centre. They would then place them on the horns of the best ox in the plough team and drink a toast. A century later the Twelfth Cake was covered with marzipan and icing, and upon it were placed the characters of pantomime – the king and the queen, the lover, the lady, the dandy and the captain. In 1854, Thackeray nostalgically used the Twelfth Night characters in his children's story *The Rose and the Ring*. Fashion changed. The old pantomime figures were replaced by Father Christmas, and, along with the rest of the celebrations, it was brought forward twelve days to provide a cake for Christmas Day.

And so let's all have a happy Christmas – first at church to celebrate Christ's birth, and then at home with clear conscience and strong digestion to enjoy a thumping good dinner and a tranche of the darkest, richest cake human ingenuity can devise.

CHRISTMAS: SUPPLY & DEMAND

What a lot of presents! All those parcels carefully or clumsily wrapped, all those mysterious packages which have been gathering under the Christmas tree. Some of them bought weeks ago and then hidden somewhere safe where you wouldn't forget – only you did. And then when you came upon two of them in a drawer, there they were, carefully wrapped but not labelled. All you could remember was that one was a first edition of Germaine Greer's *Female Eunuch* intended for Rowena (who is an old-fashioned feminist) and the other a box of cigars intended for Uncle Rupert (who isn't).

But the agony of waiting is almost over. Soon it will be time for the unwrapping of parcels, the disclosure of mysteries. With little shrieks of surprise and gasps of wonder we receive our gifts. Now, there is an art in giving and an art in receiving. And it is in receiving that our skills are sometimes most severely tested.

'Why?' you ask yourself as you unwrap a large pair of purple mittens, hand-knitted by an aunt in Wimbledon, '*Why?*'

But that is nothing compared with Uncle Rupert's baffled dismay as he unwraps that first edition of Germaine Greer's classic. As for Rowena – well, it will be a long time before she forgives you for inflicting upon her such a deeply wounding joke.

Christmas brings its challenges. You will not get the gifts you had hoped for, and you will get the ones you didn't. Here it is – the cliché which cannot be avoided (but that's the point of clichés, isn't it: they may be hackneyed, but they tell the truth). *It is the thought that counts.* Behind all those useless, unwanted gifts is the affection of the giver.

The aunt with her cottage industry in Wimbledon, turning out mittens for giant sloths, has done a beautiful deed in a harsh and utilitarian world. She has, against the odds, broken through the hard and unremitting cycle of supply and demand by supplying a product for which there was no demand. And for his part, her nephew must respond to her affection by valuing her kindness and being shamed by his ingratitude.

Today, throughout the world, countless groups of Christians are gathered together to do a good and gentle deed in a harsh and utilitarian world. We and they have come to offer a gift. To supply a product for which there is probably no demand.

Our birthday present to our Creator is, of course, very little when measured against his to us. We offer him this hour of worship – of praise and thanksgiving, of disciplined attention and active imagination. Our gift may be small, and like all our gifts it may be tainted by muddled motives. But if it expresses just one tiny thimbleful of obedience and affection, if our gift is made with just one fleeting moment of quiet attention to his love for each of us, then we will find kneeling space in the straw with the shepherds and the kings, and we and all our countless brothers and sisters in Christ across the world, gathered to celebrate his birth, will have given something which was not demanded; will have stepped for once out of the shadows into the light that shines out of Bethlehem – the light which no darkness can overcome: Jesus Christ our Lord.

CHRISTMAS: THE LORD OF MISRULE

Christmastide is a topsy-turvy season. Our forebears celebrated this brief interval (it used to last no longer than twelve days) when the 'Lord of Misrule' enjoyed his temporary reign. They lit up the cold, grey days at the turn of the year with a set of Christmas customs, some faintly religious, most robustly pagan, all designed to turn upside-down the conventions of life.

Kings and queens poor sheep-cotes have,
and mix with everybody.
The honest now may play the knave
and wise men play the noddy.

Depending upon your point of view it was either an innocent release of high spirits, a healthy reversal of the norms of society, or an incitement to debauchery. In many places special 'rules to order' this regime of licensed buffoonery were drawn up in mock legal documents, some of which still exist.

This kind of mayhem displeased the puritans, who outlawed it during the Commonwealth. It never fully recovered after the Restoration, and during the following centuries practically vanished. Some have seen a faint memory of the Lord of Misrule in Leech's illustration of 'The Spirit of Christmas Present' in Dickens's *Christmas Carol*. Some, too, have heard a distant echo in the 'Ho! Ho! Ho!' of Father Christmas.

The pre-Reformation Church joined in the party with its tradition of the Boy Bishop. In cathedrals a child was elected 'bishop'. He was vested in cope and mitre – some of these sets of robes have survived. He presided over special services – some Boy Bishop sermons, too, remain. To this child the real bishop and the cathedral dignitaries gave precedence. It was, of course, an elaborate game, but was not without its point.

At the heart of the Christmas Gospel is the same reversal, the same topsy-turviness. A king born in a stable. God revealed in an infant. Light shining in darkness. Kings kneeling in the straw. And then what? Well, then came another paradox. The shepherds went home. The Kings returned. The angels departed. For years the boy's birth was forgotten, allowing him to grow up in the safe obscurity of his Nazareth home. It was only long after, after his amazing, brief ministry thirty years later, after his arrest and crucifixion, after his resurrection and ascension, after the disciples had experienced Christ's presence in the bread and wine, it was only then that they found out from Mary about the stable, the star and that distant night when *silence lay over all and down from heaven leapt God's almighty Word.* God accommodated himself to his Creation in the birth of Jesus. That is the first incarnation and paradox. The second is this: he entrusted the knowledge of his birth to Mary and the tentative minds of a few disciples. Where's the sense in such a risk? Nowhere, except in his faith in humanity, his trust in you and me to respond.

O LITTLE TOWN OF BETHLEHEM

The year was 1865. It was Christmas Eve and night had fallen. A traveller on horseback was riding away from Jerusalem. As he approached the town of Bethlehem he paused at the field where the angels had appeared to the shepherds. Ahead he could see in the moonlight the huddle of small houses, a little town asleep beneath the silent stars. After a few moments he rode on and into Bethlehem.

The traveller was an American priest called Phillips Brooks. Behind him he had left his own country torn apart by four years of civil war – a war from which the widows and children of 750,000 dead soldiers would carry emotional scars for the rest of their lives.

Phillips Brooks, like so many pilgrims, marvelled at the contrast between this turbulent, riven, world of sin and the silent arrival in human hearts of the child of Bethlehem. Later, when he returned to his parish in Philadelphia he wrote the words of the hymn 'O Little Town of Bethlehem, how still we see thee lie.'

Each of us travels to Bethlehem in our own way, at our own speed, though sometimes God interferes and nudges us forwards in his own way and at his own speed. Like the shepherds, we come not entirely knowing what we will find. Perhaps not sure we will find anything more than a pretty story, but hoping we will.

Like the kings who came bearing gifts, we come encumbered. Their baggage included those mysterious gifts. We, too, come each with our own private freight: joys, sorrows, hopes, fears and, inevitably, remorse. These we lay in the straw before the child. No less precious in his eyes are they than gold, frankincense and myrrh.

And as we do, we pray in the words of that American traveller:

> *O holy child of Bethlehem descend to us, we pray;*
> *cast out our sin and enter in: be born in us today.*
> *We hear the Christmas angels the great glad tidings tell:*
> *O come to us, abide with us, our Lord Emmanuel.*

RISEN WITH HEALING IN HIS WINGS

Hail, the heaven-born Prince of Peace:
Hail, the Sun of Righteousness.
Light and life to all he brings,
risen with healing in his wings.

They saw the winged disc of the sun, that ancient symbol of divinity, carved high on the gates of Persepolis. They saw it again a year later on the walls of the temples in Egypt. Alexander's soldiers saw many strange gods as they campaigned across the lands of the Levant: Astarte in the cities of Tyre and Sidon; in Egypt the hawk-headed Horus and dog-faced Anubis; Mithras in Persia, this time a god in human form; and many others, each with his or her own story to tell.

But here was something different; a god too dazzling to look at, whose pure essence, untrammelled by human or animal form, allowed little scope for the story-teller's skill. Instead of Zeus and Juno and the rest of that rackety gang on Mt Olympus with their all too human goings-on, so easily imagined, here was – what? Here was the unimaginable source of light and life; a god without a story.

The idea of the winged disc was not new. A thousand years before Alexander's soldiers sacked Persepolis, pharaoh Amenhotep IV purged Egypt of its deities and replaced them with Aten, the one true god symbolised by a solar disc. In honour of his god he changed his name to Akhenaten and for seventeen years he promoted an austere monotheism. But the new doctrine did not catch on, and after his death his son, Tutankhamun, restored the old religion. All that remained were the carvings of the winged disc, accompanied in some cases by a pair of falcon wings to represent the all-embracing sky.

In the fifth century BC, the Hebrew prophet Malachi borrowed the idea of the winged solar disc for his final sermon. He must have been familiar with Mesopotamian culture; after all, his grandparents' generation had endured seventy years of exile in Babylon and brought back to Jerusalem the myths of the East. Even so, it was a daring piece of rhetoric to use such a visual metaphor. In Judaism, God was heard, but rarely seen, and the faithful were forbidden to bow down to any graven image, lest like the pagans they might take the symbol for the reality.

> 'The day is coming', Malachi declaimed to his complacent listeners, 'the day is coming, burning like an oven, when all the arrogant and evildoers will be stubble, the day that comes shall burn them up – but for you who revere his name, the sun of righteousness shall rise with healing in his wings.'
>
> (Malachi 4:1,2)

And now, three and a half millennia later, we sing at Christmas Charles Wesley's hymn celebrating the birth at Bethlehem of the Sun of Righteousness. What Akhenaten dreamed of and his court artists depicted, what Malachi foretold in Jerusalem, what Alexander the Great saw engraved in Persepolis, the unimaginable source of light and life became a child in Palestine.

THE JOURNEY OF THE MAGI

'It was no summer progress. A cold coming they had of it at this time of the year, just the worst time of the year to take a journey, and specially a long journey in. The ways deep, the weather sharp, the days short, the sun farthest off... the very dead of winter.'

Lancelot Andrewes, Bishop of Winchester, preached those words about the Three Kings during his Christmas sermon to King James I four hundred years ago. *'It was no summer progress.'* The bishop chose his words carefully. King James knew well the politics of the royal progress – that magnificent itinerary by which a monarch impressed his subjects. The heralds in tabards, the men-at-arms, the liveried attendants, the gorgeously costumed courtiers, the richly caparisoned horses, and the sovereign, jewelled, brocaded, powdered, and rouged in his gold and scarlet coach.

But this was no summer progress: this was the very heart of winter. Cold. Wet. Dark. *The ways deep, the weather sharp:* this was seventeenth century England, a landscape intersected by rutted tracks. The Magi had not come to impress, but to kneel humbly in the straw. T S Eliot picked up the words of Lancelot Andrewes' sermon in his poem 'The Journey of the Magi'. 'There were times', Eliot said, 'when the travellers regretted their decision made months before.' Had it all been a mistake? They remembered with nostalgia:

> *The summer palaces on slopes, the terraces,*
> *And the silken girls bringing sherbet.*

Why had they made the journey? It had not been at all easy.

> *The camels galled, sore-footed, refractory,*
> *The night fires going out, and the lack of shelters,*
> *And the cities hostile and the towns unfriendly,*
> *And the villages dirty and charging high prices.*

And still they travel on, those strange, over-dressed figures, carrying their enigmatic gifts of gold, frankincense and myrrh. For their journey is ours. Their hesitation, their wistfulness for the summer palaces, are ours, as well as their determination to keep going. All are ours as we too travel on. And what did it all amount to, that compulsion to visit Bethlehem? As one of the magi said:

> *Birth or Death?…*
> *We returned to our places, these Kingdoms,*
> *But no longer at ease here, in the old dispensation,*
> *With an alien people clutching their gods.*

Like them, we too can never again be at ease in the old dispensation. Bethlehem changes everything

CHURCH CALENDAR

Why does the Church have its own calendar? During February there is a pause in the sequence of Christian festivals; a break between Candlemas (February 2nd), which marks the end of the Christmas cycle of holy days, and Ash Wednesday, which marks the preparation for the golden sequence: Good Friday, Easter, Ascension and Pentecost. And so it seems a good time to ask, 'Why?'

It was not always thus. The early Christians knew nothing of these festivals. For them there was only one holy day in the calendar: Sunday. On that day they recalled all the events of their salvation in a single liturgical drama. The creation, the incarnation, the crucifixion, the resurrection and the outpouring of the Holy Spirit were all commemorated weekly in the great Eucharistic prayer.

At first, their calendar of worship was no more than this simple weekly cycle. Then they said, 'Why don't we make one Sunday more special than the others. The Jews have their Passover, why don't we have *our* Passover?'

At first the Christian Passover (Easter) commemorated the Passion, Crucifixion and Resurrection of Christ in one single liturgy on Easter Day. There was no Palm Sunday, no Maundy Thursday nor even Good Friday.

Then in about AD 380 someone called Egeria visited the Holy Land. By then the church in Jerusalem had rediscovered the places associated with Jesus's Passion: the house at Bethany, the route of Jesus's ride on the donkey, the upper room of the Last Supper, the Garden of Gethsemane, Golgotha, the Tomb. Egeria joined in the local processions and ceremonies attached to the different sites. Easter was now kept in Jerusalem not as a single day, but as an eight-day festival. Egeria kept a journal, and when she got home, she told all her friends. And so Holy Week arrived in Europe.

And with it came a shift in the focus of worship. Alongside the single celebration of our redemption (entire and complete at every Eucharist, as it still is) there arose a desire to replicate the drama of the Gospel chronologically; to recreate an historical sequence and to participate in it as if we were there with Jesus and his disciples.

Unlike Easter and Holy Week, which can be recreated in real time and whose dates are linked approximately to the Passover, Christmas is a *theological* festival. Its date (the winter solstice, near enough) and the sequence of its associated holy days (the massacre of the Innocents, the Epiphany, Candlemas) are not chosen to replicate history, but to demonstrate aspects of doctrine. That is not to say that those events did not happen, but they did not happen on those dates or even in that order. Chronology is not an issue at Christmas. In the Easter/ Pentecost cycle of feast days it is.

So why do we bother? If so much of our church calendar is chronologically wrong, why not return to the custom of the primitive church: scrap the annual cycle of fasts and festivals, and keep to the simple weekly cycle with the one, single day of celebration: Sunday. Well, the English Puritans did just that. In the days of Oliver Cromwell Christmas was cancelled, and so was much of the rest of the church's calendar. You can imagine how popular that was. It meant that the congregations were now at the mercy of the clergy. Without the structure of the Prayer Book calendar (and set readings and prayers to fit each Sunday and Holy Day) the ministers were left to their own devices. And what a disaster *that* was.

Luckily this experiment failed and the *Book of Common Prayer* and the church's calendar were restored. Since then, the *Prayer Book* and the recent provisions of *Common Worship* continue to guarantee that our congregations are nourished by a balanced diet. This means that the entire Gospel is proclaimed across the annual cycle of the calendar, and we are protected from the whims and hobby-horses of theological fashion and eccentric clergy!

WAITING FOR THE LAST CALL

What on earth is the point of February? You may well ask. It has, it seems, no greater merit than its own brevity. Of course, if your birthday falls within its short span that will be enough in your eyes to redeem its reputation. For most of us, these four dismal weeks, the fag-end of winter, serve only as a time of waiting for nature to wake up and life to start again.

However, as every mother knows, times of waiting, tedious as they may be, are part of life. Nine months is a sizeable chunk of time to have to wait. From the moment of conception to the time of birth the miraculous development within continues at its own unhurried and mysterious pace.

'Let nature take its course,' we say, and tacitly accept that there are periods in our lives when we simply have to wait. No amount of effort, interference or agitation is going to make a ha'penny's worth of difference. But the waiting does not always end in joy. 'They also serve who only stand and wait', wrote Milton about his blindness. For a scholar and poet who lived by his pen, it was a hard lesson to have to learn.

'God's waiting room' is not a bad description of the care home that, for most of us, will be our last address on earth. Waiting for that last call is going to be a severe test, and there is no knowing how you and I will cope with loss of independence. 'Rage, rage against the dying of the light', wrote Dylan Thomas to his dying father, but rage never did anyone any good. There are other ways. The human spirit is stronger than the body it inhabits, and devises little stratagems by which it might accommodate itself to the body's failing powers.

I sat in my father-in-law's room as he finished dressing.

He was nearly ninety-nine years old, and his morning routine of first selecting and then putting on his clothes was an immense and long drawn out labour, which he addressed with as much concentration and skill and effort that only four years ago he had spent upon his kitchen garden. Dressing for most of us is what we do before we start our day. But the time will come when it *is* our day. To watch him tie his tie (always a jacket and tie man) was to see how a small unconsidered manoeuvre, which for more than ninety years had lodged at the wings of his daily life, had now become a vastly complex operation at centre stage. And tying his shoe laces was another. The seven-year-old was still there; the dexterity and determination persisted.

We went down for lunch. In the lounge a dozen other residents waited to be helped into the dining room. A recording of Doris Day shook the rafters, as she belted out the 1950s hit, 'Enjoy yourself, it's later than you think; enjoy yourself, while you're still in the pink'. The listeners kept their thoughts to themselves. Later, as I drove home I pondered the great sadness of old age, but then I remembered his old hands slowly, slowly, but very deftly tying his tie, and I saw that it is by these small victories he got through the long wait for what Donne called 'the last and everlasting day'.

Perhaps, then, February does have its purpose: a bleak waiting room before the birth of Spring. Hidden, unhurried, mysterious is the pace of nature's gestation before the green shoots come breaking through. So is God's work upon each human soul, as, sooner or later, its mortal body weakens and falls away.

ASH WEDNESDAY

Remember that you are dust, and to dust you shall return.
Turn from sin and be faithful to Christ.

Those are the words spoken by the priest on Ash Wednesday as he places a smudge of ash on the foreheads of the people. It is a traditional ceremony, revived in our times as a sign of penitence.

Morbid? No, not if you consider its meaning. What is morbid is a flippant disregard of our own condition. Ash Wednesday, the first day of Lent, is an annual reminder to take ourselves seriously and to heed our final destination on this earth. *Remember that you are dust, and to dust you shall return.*

But that is not all. Dust – yes; ashes – yes; but there is hope, too; hope for us all. Without the recognition of our sinfulness, forgiveness and hope lose their power to heal. Without repentance there is no remission. Without death there is no resurrection. It is in resurrection that we believe, not immortality.

In Advent the choir sang this ancient carol; in it Our Lord utters the bleak reminder:

Remember O thou man, O thou man, O thou man,
Remember, O thou man, thy time is spent:
Remember, O thou man, how thou cam'st to me then,
And I did what I can,
Therefore repent!

The Ash Wednesday Collect, repeated daily throughout Lent, shines a bright beam of light into the dark:

Almighty and everlasting God, who hatest nothing that thou hast made, and dost forgive the sins of all them that are penitent, create and make in us new and contrite hearts.

Thomas Cranmer based this collect on the pre-Reformation prayer for blessing the ashes. Just as God lovingly created Adam from the dust of the ground, breathing into him his Holy Spirit, so he lovingly and continuously recreates us from the ashes of our lives, breathing upon us his forgiving grace.

LENT: IS LOVE ENOUGH?

'Do try to be good, dear.'

You can hear in that forlorn cry the weary tones of Joyce Grenfell reciting one of her radio monologues. As the long suffering nursery school teacher, surrounded by an invisible, but horribly real, class of unruly five-year-olds, she would plead with her little charges to be good.

'Johnny, put Lucy down... No Julia dear, not the scissors... George, don't do that.'

She conveyed a picture of the beleaguered, kindly teacher, being engulfed by a rising tide of mayhem and disaster. Eventually, and in the nick of time, she is rescued by the arrival of another, more competent, adult. 'You know,' she says sadly, as she looks at the struggling, tumbling, squabbling little heap of humanity, 'There are times when I don't think love is really enough.'

Is love enough? Is it? Well, not really. Not in human terms, that is. We need the help of rules and regulations. Without a firm structure of control we fall into all sorts of trouble. Those dark powers start to take over: faction, malice, selfishness, strife, envy, lust, rage – the whole dismal catalogue of sin.

Lent is a time to take stock of our self-imposed rules – that private code by which we try to stop our lives slipping into mayhem and disaster. The rules themselves may not matter. What does is the freedom they bring – freedom from those obstacles which stop us from being the sort of people we would like to be.

What sort of people would we like to be? Kind? Brave? Honest? Successful? Loved? Good humoured? Beautiful? Wise? Young? (aahhh). The list of qualities is endless. But it is never complete; there is always something missing. Our yearning for a better self remains unsatisfied. The sense of lost innocence lingers on. The Bible, in its oblique way, describes this yearning as our search for our true self – the Godliness or image of God in which each of us is made, and which we have smudged beyond recognition.

On Ash Wednesday the priest marks our foreheads with ash, and says, *Remember, you are dust, and to dust you shall return.* Gloomy? Not entirely. The dust from which God created Adam (you and me) he moulded into his own image. And that is the same image which he reveals in Christ, to whom he bids us return, so that: *We all... beholding the glory of the Lord, are changed into the same image from glory to glory.* (2 Cor. 3.18)

He has promised glory for us – for you and me, and for Johnny and Lucy and Julia and George. For us all his love *is* enough.

LENT: GIVING THINGS UP

Lent is once more upon us. I hope that you have not been over-zealous in your Lenten self-discipline. Modest targets are best. Queen Victoria, when told at an early age that she would one day be Queen of England, reflected upon the prospect for a moment, before saying, 'I will be good.' As a child and as an adult she was nothing if not single-minded. For her, such a bold and wide-ranging resolution – 'I will be good' – was do-able; for most of us a more specific target is needed, especially in Lent; for example: 'I will answer my emails', or 'I will be kind to so-and-so', or' I will recite psalm 121 slowly once a week' (why not?), or 'I will say once a day St Richard's prayer, and try to mean it':

> *Thanks be to Thee, my Lord Jesus Christ, for all the benefits thou hast given me, for all the pains and insults thou hast borne for me. O most merciful Redeemer, Friend and Brother, may I know thee more clearly, love thee more dearly, and follow thee more nearly, day by day. Amen.*

Giving up luxuries is itself of little spiritual value. I cannot really believe God is at all bothered whether or not we pour ourselves a second glass of wine, enjoy the sting of that daily dry martini, or plunge our hands once more into those gorgeous chocolates. But I do believe that he wants us to sharpen our awareness of his love for us and know his estimation of our worth. If our small indulgences obscure or dim that knowledge, then perhaps a bit of self-denial can be a good thing.

I have found that the nagging voice of conscience does

little to keep me on the straight and narrow path. If anything, it turns me right off this whole business of trying to be good. What does work for me – I know we are all different, and so it might not work for you – is the daily reminder that you and I have a special place in his divine heart of love (call it 'the scheme of things') however small or unworthy of his affection we may think ourselves to be.

St Gregory of Narek was an Armenian Orthodox monk and poet who lived in the tenth century. In his poem *Words to God from the depth of my heart* he wrote this:

> *There was a time when I did not exist, and thou hast created me;*
> *I did not beseech thee for a wish, and thou hast fulfilled it;*
> *I had not come into the light, and thou hast seen me;*
> *I had not yet appeared, and thou hast taken pity on me…*
> *With prescient eyes thou sawest the crimes of my guilty self;*
> *And yet thou hast fashioned me.*
> *And now, I who have been created by thee and saved by thee,*
> *And have been tended with such care,*
> *Let me not wholly perish by the blow of sin that is but the slanderer's invention;*
> *Let not the fog of my stubbornness triumph over thy forgiveness;*
> *Nor the hardness of my heart over thy forbearing goodness;*
> *Nor my mortal carnal-being over thy most perfect plenitude;*
> *Nor my material weakness over thine unconquerable grandeur.**

Have a fruitful Lent.

---

* (*Lamentations of Narek* translated by Mischa Kudian 1977, Mashtots Press, London © Mischa Kudian 1977)

LENT: A TIME FOR UNTYING THE KNOTS

St Basil the Great had some wise words to say about Lenten fasting:

Do not limit the benefit of fasting merely to abstinence from food, for a true fast means refraining from evil. Loose every unjust bond, put away your resentment against your neighbour, forgive him his offences.

He wrote those words sixteen hundred years ago, but nothing changes. Resentment of one sort or another remains a corrosive evil in our lives, 'an unjust bond'.

Resentment ties us up in knots. At worst it can seriously cripple our lives, injuring not only ourselves, but those around us. How hard we find it to untangle ourselves from our own anger at past injuries, real or imagined. At best it can turn us into petulant bores: always grumbling about some petty grievance or other, and driving our nearest and dearest mad.

I used to find myself getting enraged by a particular TV weather forecaster, until, that is, I was firmly told to shut up. The rebuke was deserved: the knot was cut. I learnt to watch Siân Lloyd in a reasonable, almost happy, frame of mind. (Sorry, Siân; I hope you never read this).

Being untied, or released from anger (and that usually means being liberated from the past) is what enables us to grow, to move forward. And that is as true of communities and nations as it is of individuals. Personally, I love the past. I am absorbed by TV documentaries about history. I believe that valuing our past (and that means cherishing the good things and coming to terms with the bad) is necessary for healthy growth. But we do need to be free of the past, not enslaved by it.

We need to be released from the unjust bonds of resentment or guilt. Repentance means a quiet turning away from our own faults and the faults of others – not a constant scratching at the sore, nor an obsessive and continuous returning to the scene of the crime.

If we believe that we are the aggrieved victim of an historic offence, extracting a public apology does nothing to advance repentance or forgiveness, but only serves to perpetuate resentment and guilt, opening afresh an ancient wound.

God has promised us that he is ready to absolve us (untie us), but we have to allow him to do it. We have to let go of our past. Then we can go forward. Then we can grow.

PRAYER IN LENT: THE SOUL IN PARAPHRASE

'*All lost! To prayers, to prayers! All lost!*' So cried the mariners in the opening scene of 'The Tempest' as their ship broke to pieces in the storm. Our response in great danger is to turn to prayer as the last resort. 'Please, God, help me; save me from this death.' So closely bound is the notion of prayer with fear of disaster that the promise to a sick friend to pray for them is often seen as an unwelcome intervention. 'Pray?,' the patient whispers hoarsely, clutching at your sleeve, '*Is it as bad as that?*'

But here is quite a different notion:

> *Prayer the church's banquet, angel's age,*
> *God's breath in man returning to his birth,*
> *The soul in paraphrase, heart in pilgrimage,*
> *The Christian plummet sounding heav'n and earth*
> *Engine against th' Almighty, sinner's tow'r,*
> *Reversed thunder, Christ-side-piercing spear,*
> *The six-days world transposing in an hour,*
> *A kind of tune, which all things hear and fear;*
> *Softness, and peace, and joy, and love, and bliss,*
> *Exalted manna, gladness of the best,*
> *Heaven in ordinary, man well drest,*
> *The milky way, the bird of Paradise,*
> *Church-bells beyond the stars heard, the soul's blood,*
> *The land of spices; something understood.*

Those words were written by the poet and priest George Herbert (1593-1633). Prayer is 'God's breath in man returning to his birth'. A thousand years earlier St Augustine had prayed,

'Thou callest us to delight in thy praise, for thou hast made us for thyself, and our hearts find no rest until we rest in thee.'

And a thousand years earlier still, Isaiah had preached to a restless people,

'In returning and rest shall ye be saved; in quietness and confidence shall be your strength.'

Lent is a time for 'returning and rest'. Not so much a period of strenuous endeavour, as a time to rediscover our true selves, to centre our wayward and fidgety beings, to find within our lives and ourselves 'Heaven in ordinary'.

THE RICH MERCHANTS OF NANTES

The rich merchants of Nantes in the eighteenth century would send their linen across the Atlantic to be laundered in the French colonies of Martinique and St Dominique where the mountain streams washed whiter than the rivers of Brittany. They could afford such luxury. Their beautiful homes and fastidious manners, like those of the merchants of Liverpool and Bristol, were founded upon the slave trade, of which their cities were the leading centres.

If you lived two hundred and fifty years ago, and if you enjoyed coffee or chocolate, you could not avoid being an accessory to the slave trade every time you raised a delicate porcelain cup to your lips, and if, as almost certainly you did, you took sugar, you were guilty twice over.

Sir Thomas Bertram of Mansfield Park was able to keep Lady Bertram – and, of course, Aunt Norris – in elegant style, because of his plantations, worked by slaves, in the West Indies. Jane Austen did not labour the point; it was, after all, a commonplace of her world.

The slave trade, which the British Parliament outlawed in 1807, was an abominable business in which most of society was implicated. It was, therefore, an astonishing achievement that the Bill was passed (in the Lords 100 to 34; in the Commons 283 to 16), given that a high proportion of members had benefited from the trade. But until Parliament acted, what could the ordinary citizen do to purge his guilt? Give up coffee? Take one spoonful of sugar instead of two? Such gestures, we may think, would be empty, hypocritical, meaningless.

Even so, little gestures of private regret are sometimes all that an individual can do. They need not be empty. They need not be hypocritical. We are now in Lent, a season of penitence, a time for gestures of private regret and self-denial. Giving up coffee or taking one spoonful of sugar instead of two may be of little or no spiritual value, but at least it foreshadows our need of greater self-discipline in a culture of self-indulgence.

To set aside three minutes each day of conscious silence may seem a poor substitute for regular devotion, but at least it reminds us how dangerous to the soul is the constant noise of our own speaking, doing, thinking. A deliberate pause is a gesture of freedom against our own inner enslavement – a small contribution to that final emancipation won for each of us by Christ.

CHRIST ON THE CROSS
TEARS UP THE CONTRACT

Ours is a compensation culture. You know how it is: *A* provides a service to *B;* the service fails to satisfy *B*; *B* claims breach of contract, and sues *A* for compensation.

Some years ago a group of American citizens, in a light-hearted moment, wrote to the Whitechapel Bell Foundry in London informing them that the Liberty Bell, cast in London in 1753, had cracked on its first being rung that year in Philadelphia (which it had). The bell was plainly 'not fit for purpose'. Would the makers of the bell please pay the State of Pennsylvania due compensation? Of course, came the reply, the company would be happy to fulfil its obligation (even though the claim was two hundred years late), but please would the State of Pennsylvania comply with *their* contractual obligation to return the damaged goods in the original packaging.

The principle of contract is one that has served mankind well for centuries. Commerce, retail, employment, marriage, and the game of bridge are based upon contracts. And so was religion once, or, at least in its more primitive aspect. God undertook to protect his people: his people undertook to obey their God. But this crudely mechanical view of life failed to do justice to all those qualities which, like love, friendship, loyalty, kindness, unselfishness, generosity and forgiveness, make life worth living. It also failed to take into account man's inability to keep his side of the agreement.

And so Jesus tore up the contract and climbed the scaffold at the place of execution.

His willing submission to our malice drew the poison of human evil. '*My people, my people, what have I done to you, how have I offended you?'* are words often sung on Good Friday. *'Is it nothing to you, all ye that pass by?'* The question hangs unanswered beneath a darkened sky. But it needs no intervention, no melodramatic transformation scene or creaking *deus ex machina* to rescue the victim. The victory is in the dying and in the loving. In St Paul's words Christ erased the broken contract, *'setting it aside, nailing it to the cross'.* (Colossians 2:14)

Easter does not cancel Good Friday. The risen Christ carries the scars of victory. The suffering was not obliterated, but transfigured in glory, so that our pain too might be transfigured by hope.

EASTER: DEATH'S DREAD STING IS DRAWN

There is a hard edge to Charles Wesley's Easter hymn:

Love's redeeming work is done
Fought the fight, the battle won:
Lo! our Sun's eclipse is o'er;
Lo! He sets in blood no more.
Vain the stone, the watch, the seal;
Christ has burst the gates of hell!
Death in vain forbids His rise:
Christ has opened Paradise.

That brisk sequence of short, sharp words packs a hard punch: *vain... stone... watch... seal... Christ... burst... gates... hell.* There's no mealy-mouthed shilly-shallying here, no gentle blurring of the sharp edges, no discreet air-brushing of the raw truth lest it offend the sensibilities of a faithless age. And the truth? Nothing less than this: that Christ died on a cross, his body was buried in a sealed tomb, he rose again on the third day, and is alive, here, now and ever.

You will notice that in nearly every hymn we sing on Easter Day death's dread sting is faced squarely, not glossed over, not diminished. The brutal reality of death, which includes the grief of bereavement, is central to the Christian belief in resurrection. It is resurrection we believe in, not immortality. When the risen Jesus appeared to his disciples, it was to the marks of his dying (his wounds) that he drew their attention. When he ate supper at Emmaus on the evening of that first Easter Day, it was by the symbols of his death (the bread broken, the wine outpoured) that he disclosed himself to the two friends. Easter does not cancel Good Friday; it interprets it, transforms it.

As we celebrate Christ's Resurrection on Easter Day, there will be some for whom the cross of bereavement is a recent and most grievous burden. For others the loss may not be recent, but the pain is still there, contained, but no less bitter. None of us can escape from this deeply troubled world and its sufferings. By our *Alleluias* on Easter Day we are not turning a blind eye to the darkness, but looking it square in the face, and seeing in it the figure of the dying Christ transfigured by his resurrection.

EASTER'S DATE

Easter is late this year (2011). The twenty fourth of April is almost as late as it can be. The last date on which Easter can fall is 25th April, and the earliest is 22nd March. You may wonder why the most important date in the Christian year should wander around in such a haphazard sort of way.

If you want to calculate the date of Easter, this is how you do it (in theory): start with the Spring equinox (21st March), go to the first full moon after that, then proceed to the following Sunday, and you have arrived at Easter Day. This year there was a wonderfully bright full moon on 19th March, but that was two days too early to be the paschal moon, for which we must wait until 18th April. The following Sunday will be 24th April. And so that is the date of Easter 2011. The calculation works this year, but not always. If you consult any authority on this arcane matter, you will be warned that the paschal moon is a liturgical concept which does not always correspond with the astronomical event. Not a lot of help.

To the modern mind, the whole business of paschal moons is at best an archaism, at worst an affront. Secular man likes his calendar to be tidy and free of lunar vagaries, especially if they are astronomically out of kilter. If he could, he would fix the date of Easter upon an invariable day. In fact, according to the Easter Act of 1928, Easter should fall on 'the first Sunday after the second Saturday of April' (the provisions of the Act are conditional upon the agreement of the churches, which is why they have never been put into effect). And, whilst about it, secular man would like to get rid of that other oddity – the 29th February. He likes to feel he is in control, and is irked by the fact that the earth's revolution of the sun takes 365 days plus six and a bit hours, which is why we have to add an extra day to every fourth year, but even that does not quite work out, and so every hundred years or so there has to be a further adjustment. How messy is *that!*

But there is another, deeper reason why the date of Easter is linked to the variations of the moon. The first generation of Christians understood the death and resurrection of Christ to be the new Passover. As devout Jews, Jesus and his disciples kept Passover each year to celebrate God's deliverance of his captive people through the waters of the Red Sea. At the Last Supper Jesus spoke of the Passover meal in terms that identified his approaching sacrifice with the paschal lamb ('This is my body broken for you... this is my blood shed for you'). Many European languages call Easter by a version of the Greek word (Pascha) which itself translates the Hebrew word for Passover (Pesach). We get our word 'paschal' from the same source. The dating of Pesach depends ultimately upon the metonic cycle of the moon (don't ask) and the Christian Church adopted a similar, but not identical practice, which means that Jewish Passover and Christian Easter do not always coincide (though this year they do).

It would be so much more convenient to fix Easter on the first Sunday after the second Saturday of April, but it would be most regrettable. These quirks of custom and language tie us to our Biblical roots – roots which grow deep into the story of the human race, and deep into the fabric and motion of the earth, sun, moon and stars, those stubborn elements that shape our calendar and all the greater and lesser occasions of our life. It is within that time-space continuum of the universe that our Creator worked his redemption of the human race by submitting to his own cosmic ordinances and by dying and rising at a date determined by the lunar cycle.

TRIP HAZARDS

The world swings from triumph to disaster. Our lives fly from joy to grief within the span of a single day.

We should be conditioned to such reverses, but we are not. At its most trivial, life is always tripping us up. When William Wordsworth walked across Westminster Bridge one fine September day in 1802, and saw London wearing like a garment 'the beauty of the morning', he felt moved to declare:

Earth has not anything to show more fair.
Dull would he be of soul who could pass by
A sight so touching in its majesty…

But what if… what if the next moment, with his attention distracted by those 'ships, towers, domes, theatres and temples', he had caught his foot and fallen? All joy would have gone. In the place of rapture, irritation would have gripped the poet's soul, and the poem would have remained unwritten.

We are destined to trip on hazards more dangerous than bumpy pavements. That nasty little creature *sin* lurks in the undergrowth of our desires. Envy, pride, anger, lust, greed, covetousness, sloth – those old familiar seven – are ready to bring us down, and others with us, sprawling in the dust.

We need a strength greater than our own to fight our lurking devils. Down the centuries men and women have found in Christ a champion in their struggle. In the great drama of Christ's Passion, which unfolds in Holy Week, our little struggles are writ large and raised to a universal scale. Displayed for all time upon the cross is the cosmic battle between good and evil. A fifteenth century Scottish poet,

William Dunbar wrote:

Done is a battle on the dragon black
Our champion Christ confounded has his force;
The gates of hell are broken with a crack,
The sign triumphal raised is of the Cross.

Many reading this will have gone through dark times during recent months, will have had their own dragons to fight. Illness, bereavement, money problems, anxiety, failures of others, failures of their own, or just a long drawn out weariness of spirit. For many people life does indeed swing from joy to grief, as surely as the day gives way to night. But the Easter message is and continues to be this: that contrary to all expectation the sleepless night gives way to day, and our darkness is at last dispelled by light.

ASCENSION DAY

Ascension Day falls forty days after Easter Day. There is a symmetry here between the two great festivals of the Christian year: Christmas and Easter. Each season of forty days concludes with a festival: Candlemas and Ascension Day.

On the Continent – even in those nations like France which have long ago dissolved all formal links between church and state – Ascension Day is still kept as a public holiday. In England we are more reticent about observing religious festivals (which is a polite way of putting it), though there still linger distant memories of marking the Ascension of Our Lord with a day off school, and, if you wake early enough, you may hear sung briefly on Radio Four the Ascension Day hymn, before John Humphrys sets about his daily task.

Observing religious festivals with a holiday can have unexpected results. Evelyn Waugh, as a thirteen-year-old pupil at Lancing, found himself turned out of doors, and crying alone and friendless on the rain-swept Sussex Downs. Saints' days were observed by giving the boys a half-holiday. Ascension Day was kept as a whole-holiday, the school was closed and the boys dispersed. No one had told young Waugh. As an adult he always remembered to pray on Ascension Day for desolate children.

Not so long ago – and it still happens in some more remote parishes – the day was marked by 'beating the bounds'. In other parishes beating the bounds took place in Rogationtide. According to this ancient custom the parson, churchwardens and other assorted worthies would walk the boys of the village round the parish boundaries, stopping at certain landmarks – a spring or mill or ancient oak. Here they would tell the boys to beat the ground with willow wands to implant in the memory of the next generation the exact line of the parish bounds. In some parishes, by way of encouragement, they beat the boys as well.

None of which, you might say, has much to do with the Ascension of Our Lord, although, as with so much of our calendar, these oddities serve to remind us that religious practice and secular practicality (boundaries *are* important) are enmeshed together in our lives. And that should come as no surprise to believers in Jesus Christ, in whom God and Man, sacred and secular, are so closely interwoven that when at his ascension he took with him his transformed and risen body into heaven, he took also our humanity in which he shared. He broke the bounds of earth and heaven.

THE FATAL BELLMAN

Cutting through the music on my headphones came the voice of doom:

BASINGSTOKE. THIS IS BASINGSTOKE.

The pretty strains of Mozart's 'Eine Kleine Nachtmusik' were drowned out by the repeated warning. Even the chirpy voice on the train's PA system, with its repeated assurance that our final destination was Bristol Temple Meads, now fell silent. The train had stopped.

BASINGSTOKE. THIS IS BASINGSTOKE.

But no one got out. No one got in.

The young woman sitting next to me did not look up, but continued to play her laptop keyboard, her deft fingers brushing silently and swiftly across the keys. She had been doing this without a break since Waterloo. By covertly swivelling my eyes I had been able to make out the figures and graphs on her screen. She was working on her dissertation on the demography of popular sport in contemporary Britain. I was able to make out the title in bold capitals.

Beyond her was a mother and two young children, both of whom were clicking their mobiles, engrossed in their internet games. The mother looked up momentarily from her copy of *Hello,* before returning to read more about a pop-star's mansion in Esher.

Opposite me an elderly man slept, his hat tilted over his eyes. Earlier he had begun to snore, which made the children giggle and whisper. What if this was his station? Should I rouse him? As if reading my thoughts, he stirred, peered through the window, sighed, wriggled into a more comfortable position and went back to sleep.

In my headphones Classic FM had now moved on from Mozart to Franz Lehar. In the present circumstances the Merry Widow waltz sounded absurdly frivolous.

BASINGSTOKE. THIS IS BASINGSTOKE.

Again that doleful call. Was it summons or warning?

In the old days the night-watchman called out the passing hours of darkness in just such doleful tones. To add emphasis he would ring his bell. The sleeping citizens of London – among them Dr Donne, who next day was due to preach before the king – stirred, turned over and sunk back into their pillows. But the sound of the bellman would enter and echo in their memory throughout the following day; a melancholy bourdon beneath the noise of their daily lives.

The bellman entered Donne's sermon too. 'Remember' he warned the royal household that Sunday morning in the palace chapel, 'Remember as you hear cheerful street music in the winter mornings, yet there was a sad and doleful bellman that waked you and called upon you two or three hours before that music came; so for all that blessed music which the servants of God (the choir of the Chapel Royal) shall present to you in this place, it may be of use, that a poor bellman waked you before, and though but by his noise, prepared you for his music.'

The train moved off. For us travellers – for the sleeping man in his tilted hat, for the postgraduate student, for the mother, her children and for me, a retired cleric on a necessary and unwelcome journey – for us all the music of our daily lives played on, but always beneath our little tunes there would continue to sound a deeper note, the fatal bellman's melancholy call, preparing our souls for a music more glorious, more enduring and more complete.

THE INSTABILITY OF WORDS

Words are slippery, fluid,unstable. We try to fix them, lest there should be any doubt about their meaning. That is probably why on solemn occasions we duplicate them in an attempt to pin the little brutes down. Look at the terms of the contract by which a couple vow *'to have and to hold'* each other in wedlock, but not before the banns have been called inviting anyone to declare if he knows of *'any cause or just impediment'* why the marriage should not take place. Then many years later (and one must hope very many years later) when *'death doth them part'* the late lamented is found to have left *'a last will and testament'*.

To leave the terminology in the singular and unsupported by its partner might invite trouble in the future. Who is to say that those neat, tidy, and apparently well-behaved little words *'have'*, *'cause'* and *'will'* might not some day scamper off, mix with the wrong company, pick up bad habits and quite alter their meaning, were they not kept in check by their companions *'hold'*, *'impediment'* and *'testament'*?

'Comfort' is a case in point. It used to be such a strong word, its sense linked to 'fortitude'. When the bride and groom promise to comfort one another they are undertaking to strengthen each other in moments of weakness, not indulge each other. The Holy Spirit of God is sometimes called in the Bible 'The Comforter'. At Whitsun the Church celebrates the occasion when the Holy Spirit came down upon the apostles with such power that the room they were in shook as if a gale was blowing and flames of fire seemed to be flickering over their heads. Not a comfortable experience in the modern sense of the word.

Religion is often spoken of as a comfort. And that is true. The Good Samaritan, who is Jesus Christ, pours oil on our wounds. But he also pours on vinegar. The disinfectant property of his healing love stings. Ours is not an easy calling. The language of Baptism speaks about dying and rising with Christ. Jesus himself talked about taking up our cross to follow him. Whitsun (Pentecost) teaches us that Our Lord is present in our lives through his Holy Spirit to strengthen our weak wills and embolden us so that we can live up to our baptismal promise.

OLD TOBY'S DRY MARTINI

'Great Scott', wheezed Toby, 'What in heaven's name is *that*?'

Toby is an old and rather disreputable curmudgeon (but a dear friend notwithstanding) who is convinced that the whole world is in conspiracy to ruin his peace of mind. It began with decimal coinage. Then came centigrade. 'Good grief, woman, what's wrong with Fahrenheit?' he would bellow nightly at the TV weather forecaster. And, when once he had begun to suspect there was a plot, the evidence grew and grew. Mumbai. Beijing. Train station. *Ree*-search. Duch-*ess*. The new £20 note. Call centres. The list still grows.

The trouble this time was the shape of the bottle I had brought him. As long as Toby could remember, Noilly Prat, the French vermouth with which he flavours his six o'clock gin, had come in the same bottle. Now some bright spark in marketing had changed its shape. It was a cruel blow, and struck to the heart.

Sudden changes to the trivia of life unsettle us all. Yet at a deeper level gradual change is a necessary element in any living organism. Even Toby, who used to loathe the telephone, now enjoys his computer, and has a growing circle of on-line correspondents, all logging on to a favourite 'blog' to deplore the ghastliness of modern life and its devilish technology.

If truth be known, Toby, like Queen Victoria, is much more adaptable than he pretends. But, he would say, the most effective change must be well-rooted and continuous with the past, which is what our ancestors meant by *radical*. When Queen Victoria first travelled by rail from Windsor via Slough to Paddington, she did so with her coachman, complete in scarlet livery, standing on the footplate. Thus her courtiers preserved the continuity between horse-drawn carriage and steam-powered locomotive. Ours, after all, is an evolutionary, not a revolutionary, constitution.

The first Whit Sunday must have felt as explosive and unexpected as any new experience could possibly be: the house a-quake, the room in which the disciples sat filled with Pentecostal tongues of fire and a hurtling hurricane of wind. This was, indeed, something new: the Holy Spirit of God roaring into their lives, transforming a huddle of timid people into the bold pioneers of the Faith.

But it was also continuous with the past; with the life of Jesus Christ and with the ancient Hebrew scriptures. Our Lord had talked about the time when his spirit would be given them. And when the Spirit came, it did so in the form traditionally associated with the God of Sinai: fire and wind and terrifying power.

Life-enhancing change comes in the re-discovery of eternal truths; not in a restless tinkering with the appearance of things.

ANGELS ON PECKHAM RYE

'Be an angel, and run and tell your father that lunch is on the table.'

And for once 'angel' is the right word. The Greek *'angelos'*, from which we get our word *angel,* originally meant 'messenger'. Anyone could be an 'angelos'.

Then, in time, the messenger grew wings.

In some of the more ancient stories in the Old Testament it is not clear if the messenger is human or not. There has always been a belief that God speaks to us through the conscious, or unconscious, intervention of strangers. As St Paul wrote, 'Be not forgetful to entertain strangers; for thereby some have entertained angels unawares.'

But there is another sort of angel. One of the oldest Christian prayers, the *Sanctus,* includes the words, 'With angels and archangels, and all the company of heaven, evermore praising Thee and saying: holy, holy, holy, Lord God of hosts…'

These are the spiritual beings who surround the throne of heaven. Among them are the archangels: Gabriel who spoke to Mary; Raphael, the healer, who travelled with Tobias; Michael who slew the dragon 'that old serpent called the Devil'. Michaelmas (29th September) is the day the Church honours him and all the angels.

Our ancestors had no difficulty in believing in angels. Nor would we, if our imagination was not so impoverished by our reason.

William Blake, the painter and poet who lived two hundred years ago, and who wrote the poem we know as *Jerusalem,* was one of those people for whom heaven kept breaking in. As a child on a walk in the fields of Peckham Rye he saw a tree with branches full of angels clustered like golden birds.

As he lay dying Blake talked much about the country he was going to and which all his life he had wished to see. Just at the end his face lit up, his eyes brightened and he began to sing of the things he saw in heaven. We can be sure that, like Hamlet, 'flights of angels sang him to his rest.'

May God and his holy angels protect us all.

ALTAR OR HOLY TABLE

The design and furnishing of our parish churches tell us about our beliefs. One of the standard features of a church is the Chancel Arch, which separates nave and chancel. In some churches the 'holy end' is partly concealed behind a screen. The word 'chancel' comes from a word meaning the lattice-work screen which protected senior court officials from the intrusive stare of the crowd. Thus we have a 'Chancellor' of the Exchequer, though to what extent his work should be concealed from view is a matter of opinion.

It was also a matter of opinion that the 'holy end' of the church should *not* be hidden, and so in the sixteenth and seventeenth centuries most parish churches lost their chancel screens, and the mysteries of the Mass, now called by another name, were thrown open to full view. As part of the process of de-mystifying worship our reforming forebears broke up the stone altars and replaced them with wooden tables. At Holy Communion the table would be moved from the east end towards the middle of the church, and the communicants gathered round.

Then in 1633 came Archbishop William Laud. 'This has gone too far,' he said. 'Familiarity breeds contempt'. Or words to that effect. 'Put the altar back'. And so they did. Churchwardens were ordered to construct an altar rail. The declared reason for this was to protect the altar from being fouled by dogs (they seemed to have a lot of trouble with dogs; to beat them off churchwardens were given staves, which they carry to this day). Laud had something other than naughty dogs in mind. He knew that the rail, once secured to the floor, would prevent any disobedient clergy from ever again moving the altar away from the east end. He was only partially successful. Parliament chopped off his head, which hardly helped, and then Cromwell stabled his horses in church, which was about as far as you could go in de-mystifying any building, let alone a church.

The Cromwellian interregnum lasted barely eleven years. At the Restoration of the Monarchy the churches were restored. Then came the Age of Reason, and in the churches built during the eighteenth century chancels almost disappeared, reduced to a pretty alcove reminiscent of a feature in an Adam drawing room. Our Georgian forebears did not wish to be disturbed by the miraculous or the sacred. The pulpit replaced the altar as the focus of attention. Then a hundred years later came Newman, Keble and Pusey. Reginald Sackville-West heard them preach at Oxford. When he became Rector of Withyham in 1841 he set about restoring the chancel. The clutter of old box pews which would have obscured the altar was replaced by choir stalls, set north-south, for a robed choir. The chancel was raised a step from the nave, and the sanctuary another step higher. Once more it was the altar, raised more than a foot higher than the nave, which commanded attention, not the pulpit. A low wooden screen was put up (later removed). These and other details of furnishing were introduced to draw attention to the holiness of the sanctuary, and the separation between sacred and secular.

And so the pendulum of liturgical fashion swings reflecting two extremes: too much reason and we lose the mystery, too much mystery and we lose our reason.

AMALFI AND ST ANDREW'S BONES

We were in Amalfi, sitting on the balcony having breakfast. The view over the bay was beautiful; the sun hot; the sea enticing. It was a view which had dazzled many over the past two and a half millennia. First came the Greeks with their cultured ways, five centuries before Christ. Then the Romans, who sailed down the coast, built pretty villas and cultivated their estates, rural retreats away from the stench of the town. Byzantines from Constantinople came next, leaving, in nearby Ravello, bronze doors and mosaics, a reminder that there was once a time when most of what we now call Italy was ruled by the bureaucrats of Byzantium and the Patriarch of Constantinople.

There followed Arab merchants from Africa and the Levant who came to conquer, but stayed to trade, bringing the technique of paper manufacture and skills in navigation. Amalfi's paper mills, the first in Europe, were active until the nineteenth century, and it was one of her sons, Flavio Gioia, who invented the compass. You can still see the vaulted building where Amalfi's fleet, once greater than that of Venice, was constructed. They called it by an Arabic word: the *arsenal.*

By the fourteenth century this tiny maritime republic had seen its days of glory slip into history, leaving it as an appendage to its powerful neighbour, Naples. But still the visitors kept coming. Boccaccio, Ibsen (let's hope the experience cheered him up), Longfellow, Wagner, Grieg, Verdi and Greta Garbo. There was another visitor, greater than all these, not for what he achieved, but for whom he served: St Andrew, the first to be called by Jesus to be an apostle. His remains are buried in the crypt of Amalfi Cathedral.

The story is confused, and you might think incredible. It tells how, after his martyrdom at Patras in Greece, his body was buried in Constantinople. In 1208 his bones were stolen and divided. They were moved to various places in Europe, Rome and Amalfi claiming to be the chief venues.

There is a ghoulish aspect of relics which we find repellent. But there is also a lesson. These bits of mortality confront the believer with the actuality of the Christian Gospel. Ours is more than a religion of abstract ideas. It is grounded in real places like Bethlehem, Capernaum and Golgotha. The olive trees you can see and touch today in Gethsemane share the same genes with the ones Jesus touched and prayed beneath. The bones in that tomb in Amalfi belonged to a man who had breakfasted with Christ.

Seated on the balcony we saw the whole baggage train of history trundling past the bay of Amalfi. Standing before St Andrew's tomb we visitors from Withyham encountered at only two degrees of separation the historical figure of Jesus Christ. Makes you wonder. And *that's* the miracle.

BARNABY BRIGHT

Barnaby bright, Barnaby bright,
longest day and shortest night.

Thus our ancestors would sing on 11th June, St Barnabas' Day. Longest day? Well, at that time it *was* the longest day. Only after we had changed from the Gregorian to the Julian calendar in 1752 and had removed eleven days to bring the calendar year in line with the solar year, did mid-summer's day fall on or about 22nd June. There has always been a beguiling lack of precision in folklore about the exact date. Some stick to the solstice (21st June), others to St John the Baptist's Day (24th June, the old quarterly rent day) others to 'Old' St Barnabas' Day (22nd June, which according to one view was really the 11th, and would be so still if the government had not 'stolen' those eleven days in 1752). St. Barnabas is sometimes depicted holding a rake, because his day is, or was, during the hay harvest.

Pluie à la sainte Opportune;
il n'y a ni cerises, ni prunes.

St Opportune was a French abbess who lived in the eighth century; one of those saints who, like our St Swithin, has strong meteorological connections. If it rains on her feast day (22nd April) there will be no cherries or plums that year.

St Swithin's day, if it do rain,
for forty days it will remain.

St Swithin's day falls on 15th July. But which calendar determines the old rhyme? Julian or Gregorian? I suppose you can take your pick. If it rains on the 15th, you could always try the 26th, Old St Swithin's Day, and hope the sun shines then.

St John the Baptist is another June saint. The feast of his nativity falls on 24th This date was chosen by the early church to mark his birth because the Bible records that he was six months older than his cousin, Jesus. Why not the 25th June to match 25th December? It would have been tidier. Ah, well, there is a reason, and it has to do with the Latin method of naming the days of the month – a method which persisted into the Middle Ages.

According to this method the days of the month were not named numerically from the 1st to the 31st (or 28th, 29th or 30th as the case may be). They were named according to their position relative to the three markers which fell at fixed intervals: the *Kalends* (the 1st of the month), the *Nones* (5th or 7th depending on which month) and the *Ides* (13th or 15th). The days were reckoned in retrograde order, and so what we know as 10th March was called 'the sixth day before the Ides of March' (or *VI Id Mar*). Christmas Day was reckoned as the eighth day before the Kalends of January (*VIII Kal Jan)*. You have to start counting back from the 1st January, and so 25th December is *VIII Kal Jan,* not *VII Kal Jan*.

And so, if the Birth of Christ was to be celebrated on *VIII Kal Jan,* it followed that John the Baptist's birth should be celebrated on the corresponding day six months earlier, i.e. *VIII Kal Jul.* Of course, they knew these were arbitrary dates. They were not attempting to create an exact chronology. No one knew then and no one knows now the exact date of Christ's birth or of John's.

You will probably have spotted the flaw. *VIII Kal Jul* translated into our modern method of reckoning is not 25th June, but the 24th. The apparent symmetry between *VIII Kal*

Jan and *VIII Kal Jul* breaks down because there are 31 days in December and only 30 in June. And so that is why we celebrate the birth of John the Baptist on the 24th June instead of the 25th, which was the date originally intended.

The other date connected with 25th December is that of the Annunciation (Lady Day) which falls on 25th March. In this case the Early Church observed an exact interval of nine calendar months, and the symmetry between *VIII Kal Jan* and *VIII Kal Apr* translated into 25th December and 25th March because December and March have an equal number of days.

What does all this pedantry and idle speculation amount to? In the greater scheme of things not a jot. But then religion, with its bias towards solemnity, must have its lighter side, its harmless curiosities. Surely they must laugh as well as sing in heaven.

BEYOND THE ENCHANTED WOOD

Some years ago I went to an exhibition of the work of E H Shepard, the illustrator of A A Milne's Christopher Robin stories. It held some surprises. There were, of course, his familiar drawings of Winnie the Pooh and Piglet, but there was evidence of a darker side – hints of the wilderness that lies outside the Hundred Acre Wood, beyond Christopher Robin's 'enchanted place'.

Ernest Shepard won the Military Cross in the First World War, and commanded a section of the Home Guard in the Second. One of the exhibits was the map which he drew in the course of his war duties, showing the Surrey hills complete with gun emplacements. This map, drawn in the same style as his illustration of the Hundred Acre Wood, is a forceful reminder that our enchanted landscape conceals within it the grim horrors of human destruction.

There, too, were his first pictures of Christopher Robin. Shepard used as his model his own son, Graham, who was later killed in a naval engagement at sea in the Second World War.

Sombre thoughts for summer. It now seems inconceivable that our hills and woods and commons could ever be the scene of battle; that the long meadow grass, and the hedgerows full of dog roses and birdsong could ever be scorched and flattened by war. For 350 years our countryside has been safe; war, we are led to believe, happens abroad.

But war always happens at home, though it may not be ours. And those ugly concrete 'pill boxes' which survive in the fields remind us that it could have been, and very nearly was.

Most land battles have been fought in high summer, at

that time of year when nature is at her most beautiful, and life is most sweet… Waterloo, the Boyne, the Somme. We kill each other when the grass is lush and the roses are in bloom.

This terrible irony, that within the enchantment of the Hundred Acre Wood there lurks the serpent of destruction, is one of the oldest truths known to man. It is there in the story of Adam and Eve.

Enchanted places serve for our delight and our refreshment, but they provide us with no lasting home. Beyond the Hundred Acre Wood lies the grown-up world with its loveliness and its cruelties. It is out there that we live. It is out there that the Cross impinges.

BREAKING DOWN THE BARRIERS

There is a story that when King Richard I fell seriously ill during the Third Crusade, Saladin, 'The Sword of Islam', sent his Jewish physician, Maimonides, to heal the Christian king. The legend testifies to the possibility, at least, of Jewish, Christian and Muslim co-operation. In the Levant, the birthplace of the world's three great monotheistic religions, there have been times of co-existence and mutual respect, as well as times of murderous intolerance. The tragedy of our age is that not only the Middle East, but much of the rest of the world too, is plunged into a period of interfaith hatred. It was not always thus, nor need it be.

One of the virtues of history is that a study of the past shows that what once seemed unchangeable in our broken world *can* be changed. The slave trade, once an essential part of the British economy, was abolished. The nations of Europe, at war with each other for a thousand years, now live in peace. The Berlin Wall came down. One week it was there, immoveable, permanent – the next week it had crumbled. In Northern Ireland, Ian Paisley and Martin McGuinness shook hands and shared power. In South Africa the evil apparatus of apartheid was dismantled, and the prisoners of Robben Island set free.

Appalling atrocities, in the name of religion and tribal loyalty, continue to threaten the peace negotiations, currently, and often inconspicuously being carried on behind the smokescreen of battle. The worst thing we can do is give up hope, give up our belief that things *can* be changed for the good, however distant that prospect may be. Over and over again the stories of the Old Testament of the Bible (shared by Jew, Christian and Muslim) hammer home the point that human goodness, with the grace of God, can prevail over human evil. Men will turn their swords into ploughshares and their spears into pruning hooks.

There is much, you might say too much, about war in the Bible, but there is also a great deal about peace. The golden age for the ancient Israelites was not the reign of their warrior king David, but the reign of his son Solomon. Solomon's success was founded upon commerce and trade, the twin fruits of peace and her most powerful agents, creating a climate in which the arts, architecture, scholarship and religion could flourish.

Commerce and trade build surprising bridges. In twelfth century Cairo, at that time the world's largest city, shared ownership of properties crossed confessional boundaries. Business partnerships linking Jew, Christian and Muslim were commonplace. Documents survive that show that such partnerships were registered at Muslim and rabbinic courts.

Peace is won by compromise, self-interest, 'realpolitik', armed force, vigilance, low cunning and weary determination. No doubt about that. But also needed are forgiveness and hope and an unshakeable belief that things can change, that the walls of hatred, against all the odds, can and will come down.

BROWN ALE: OH, THE DISGRACE!

The Headmaster was looking exceptionally severe. The boys of the King's School had been assembled in the ancient Chapter House of Canterbury Cathedral. They knew what was coming. After a suitably august pre-amble, Canon Shirley announced in tones of sorrow mingled with shock that two members of the oldest and finest school in the kingdom had been observed by a member of the public 'in a railway carriage, drinking what appeared to be brown ale from the bottle.' He paused and shook his head in disbelief. 'Gentlemen – *brown ale...*' pause...*'from the bottle?'* Then he gathered his gown around him and swept out in silence. It was a moment of great theatre. The culprits were left to face the withering scorn of their peers. That was punishment enough.

There is often utter disparity between the offence committed and the shame of disclosure. The consequence of our discovered misdemeanours, expressed in the embarrassment we feel and the reproach we may endure, is sometimes entirely disproportionate to the gravity of the offence. It is a question of brown ale. The reasons why we are so ashamed of quite trivial shortcomings, and yet not in the least embarrassed by more serious ones are quite arbitrary. In the days of Oliver Cromwell, clergy were deprived of their office for frequenting playhouses, wearing surplices and 'scandalously eating custard', but not for preaching rotten sermons or neglecting their flock.

Religion is inclined to heap up guilt by creating all sorts of categories of sin, some of which you might never think of committing. The Bible – particularly the Old Testament – is full of strange and undreamt-of offences. Although supping custard (scandalously or otherwise) is not among them, eating hoopoes is. And so is marrying a foreigner. And so is travelling on the Sabbath.

But though the Bible inhibits and restricts, the Bible also liberates. Jesus's words, as recorded in the New Testament, go back to the two basic rules of the Jewish faith: love God and love your neighbour. *'On these two commandments hang all the Law and the Prophets,'* he said. By the phrase 'the Law and the Prophets' he meant the whole tradition of his religion. It was his radical attitude to that tradition (his return to the *roots*) that provoked the authorities to have him arrested and killed.

BURIAL IN A COUNTRY CHURCHYARD

Man that is born of a woman hath but a short time to live, and is full of misery. He cometh up, and is cut down, like a flower; he fleeth as it were a shadow, and never continueth in one stay.

In the midst of life we are in death: of whom may we seek for succour, but of thee, O Lord, who for our sins art justly displeased?

Yet, O Lord God most holy, O Lord most mighty, O holy and most merciful Saviour, deliver us not into the bitter pains of eternal death.

Thou knowest, Lord, the secrets of our hearts; shut not thy merciful ears to our prayer; but spare us, Lord most holy, O God most mighty, O holy and merciful Saviour, thou most worthy Judge eternal, suffer us not, at our last hour, for any pains of death, to fall from thee.

(From the Burial Service in the Book of Common Prayer)

The cortège moves uncertainly through the churchyard, the elderly pall-bearers lurching over the uneven ground. After the prayers and the hymns, after the tribute with its anecdotes and uneasy jokes, after the bible-reading and the poem and the sermon, after the commendation and the affirmation of hope, after the beautiful and measured liturgy of the church, comes this: a tidying away of the mortal remains.

But first these words:

Man that is born of a woman hath but a short time to live, and is full of misery. He cometh up, and is cut down, like a flower; he fleeth as it were a shadow, and never continueth in one stay.

71

It is a windy day and a gust snatches Job's words from my mouth. I do my best to be audible, and think of Ken's ninety-three years and my own seventy-five. The men are muttering and struggling to lower the coffin into the grave.

In the midst of life we are in death. Notker, a ninth century monk, wrote those words, inspired by the sight of workmen building a bridge, suspended high above a mountain gorge in his native Switzerland. What if those men should lose their hold and fall. Such tiny helpless figures, spinning through vast eternity. Like Shakespeare's samphire-gatherer clinging to the cliff high above Dover beach. Like those men and women, some still clutching their briefcases, falling and falling from the twin towers of the World Trade Centre. *Lord God most holy, Lord most mighty, O holy and most merciful Saviour, deliver us not into the bitter pain of eternal death.* The words of the Trisagion were already ancient before Notker included them in his prayer.

I say the words of committal, *earth to earth, ashes to ashes, dust to dust,* and cast earth upon the coffin. Then a prayer and it is all over. There is a pause. I know Derek, the gravedigger, is standing out of sight behind some bushes, waiting to do his work. I cannot see him, but a whiff of smoke from his straggly roll-up signals his presence. I hold the pause a little longer.

> *Lord, thou knowest the secrets of our hearts* (the words are Luther's) *spare us, most worthy judge eternal; at our last hour let us not fall from you.*

What if at my last hour I for the pains of death should lose my hold and fall? Pray for us, Mary, pray for us sinners now and at the hour of our death.

We move away, rather uneasily, not wishing to intrude upon the family's grief, but not wanting to ignore it either. 'Do you all know the way to the village hall?' says someone. 'Does anyone want a lift?' asks someone else, 'I've got room for two.' Over tea and sandwiches we recover our composure and talk of this and that. We, who have seen the doors opening and felt the draught in our face, have no words of our own commensurate with the solemn mystery of death, but we have the words of others; of Job and of the ancient liturgy of Constantinople, of Notker, the medieval monk and of Martin Luther, too. Words strong enough to bear the weight of death.

CHRISTIAN SYMBOLS

 The earliest Christian symbol was a fish scratched on catacomb walls in ancient Rome. It is thought to have been used as a secret sign by the Early Church in times of persecution, and derives from an acrostic from the Greek word ἰχθυς (ichthus=fish), the five Greek letters are the intials of the Greek for 'Jesus Christ, Son of God, Saviour'.

 'In this sign thou shalt conquer'. Those were the words the Emperor Constantine heard on 28th October, AD 312, as he saw in the sky the ancient Christian monogram (the Chi Ro) depicting the first two letters of the Greek word χριστος (Christos). According to legend this happened just before he defeated Maxentius at the Battle of the Milvian Bridge, thereby becoming undisputed Emperor of the Roman Empire. The event led to his conversion to Christianity and its establishment as the official religion of the Empire. The Greek letter for 'Ch' (as in 'chorus') was sometimes used as an abbreviation of 'Christ' (as in Xmas).

 The letters INRI referring to the Passion of Our Lord and used in art and on church embroidery, are the initials of the four Latin words which Pilate ordered to be placed upon the Cross: Iesus Nazarenus Rex Iudaeorum (Jesus of Nazareth King of the Jews).

† But, of course, it is the Cross itself which has become the universally recognised symbol of our Faith. We are baptised with the sign of the Cross. A priest blesses us and pronounces absolution with the sign of the Cross. Christians at prayer make the sign of the Cross (in the Catholic West, which includes us Anglicans, we cross ourselves from left to right; in the Orthodox East they cross themselves from right to left).

So widely used has this sacred sign become that its meaning is often lost. Even so, we should not be offended when athletes and footballers cross themselves, as they sometimes do, before running a race or taking a penalty kick, though the spectacle of the badge of Christ's cosmic victory reduced to a lucky charm may raise a quizzical eyebrow in heaven. Nor should we be so churlish as to cavil at the sight of a jewelled cross upon a lady's necklace. Surely the irony of turning an instrument of death into a beautiful ornament is not lost on the Saviour who died on that same Cross to save us all. Besides, it is not charitable, nor is it wise, to cast doubts upon the sincerity of another's faith. The late Tsarina of all the Russias at dinner in full fig may indeed have worn a diamond-encrusted Fabergé cross, but none could doubt the devotion she gave her crucified Lord.

Of the compelling power of his death on the Cross Jesus said, '*I, if I am lifted up, will draw all men unto me,*' but he also said, '*If any man will come after me, let him deny himself, and take up his cross, and follow me.*' Good Friday challenges us all to take seriously his Cross and ours.

THE WONDERFUL COHERENCE OF CREATION

In his TV series, *Wonders of the Universe*, Professor Brian Cox showed that each of us is made of the same material as the oldest rocks on our planet and as the furthest stars of our universe. Physical matter is constructed from a tiny collection of basic ingredients, assembled in a staggering variety of permutations. From this glorious mélange come earth, stone, wood, water, blood, hair, skin, teeth, bone, you, me. 'Ultimately', he said, 'we are part of the universe.' Now, I find that a delightful thought. I can say to my fingers and toes, those uncomplaining friends of more than seventy years, 'Look at the stars, you little people, look at the hills; they are your brothers, they are your sisters'.

St Francis had the same vision as Brian Cox. In his 'Canticle of the Sun', written in 1224, he sings of Brother Sun and Sister Moon, of Brother Fire and Sister Water (we sing a modern version of this in the hymn 'All creatures of our God and King'). Mystic and physicist, saint and scientist, approach the same truth from different directions. How silly we are to set up science against faith, when the same sense of breathless wonder holds them both in rapture as they contemplate the glory of the universe.

William Blake managed, during a long life, to write a great deal of nonsense, but amongst it some wonderfully perceptive lines. He lamented the breaking of the spiritual bond which tied humanity to the rest of creation, and which had shaped Judaeo-Christian thought for centuries. For this disintegration he blamed Isaac Newton and the Enlightenment. The spiritual coherence of creation, observed by the Hebrew prophets, celebrated by St Paul in his letter to the Colossians (ch.1: 15-

20), acclaimed by the Church in that great hymn, the *Benedicite Omnia Opera,* had now been split into its component parts, each fragment alienated from the other and trapped in its own singularity: body versus soul, mind versus matter, animate versus inanimate. For Blake, the schools and universities of Europe were the dark satanic mills upon whose looms was woven the new analytical philosophy which –

'Separated the stars from the mountains, the mountains from man,
And left man a little grovelling root outside of himself.'

It was Blake's mission to re-connect heart and mind, humanity and creation. His was a mental fight to build again Jerusalem in England's green and pleasant land. Nothing to do with the smoking chimneys of factories or the preservation of rural England, but everything to do with the recovery of that vision of coherence and of wholeness which Brian Cox and St Francis reveal to us in the universe, and which the Bible locates in the New Jerusalem, the home of a redeemed and healed humanity.

DIEU ME PARDONNERA: C'EST SON MÉTIER

'Dieu me pardonnera; c'est son métier', sighed the poet Heinrich Heine on his death bed. 'God will forgive me; it's his job.'

An over-familiarity with the Almighty is, I suppose, the down-side of a Gospel that teaches us that God's love for us is unconditional; unconditional, that is, on his part, but not unconditional on ours. It is our rejection of it – complete or partial – that blocks the flow of his forgiveness. The lock, after all, is on our side of the door.

Forgive us our trespasses, as we forgive those who trespass against us – words so well-known to us from the Lord's Prayer – do not mean that our Father desires to hold back – that he grudgingly balances his distribution of love to us against our record of generosity to others. The words mean, rather, that only when we open ourselves to him unconditionally can we receive his gift in its fullness, and part of that opening-up involves our forgiveness of others. It is we who set the limits, not God.

In a moving outburst, Jesus describes his love for us as that of a mother-hen for her little chicks: *'O Jerusalem, Jerusalem… how often would I have gathered thy children together, as a hen doth gather her brood under her wings, and ye would not.'*

Now here is the hard bit. How do I forgive someone who has hurt me – or, more to the point, has hurt someone I love – so badly, that a ready forgiveness on my part runs the risk of trivialising the offence and betraying the victim? Sometimes, for us, reconciliation is impossible. The phrase *as we forgive those who trespass against us* then becomes not so much a statement of virtuous achievement as an admission of failure.

For those of us who live in the knowledge that we can never entirely forgive, help is at hand. It is Christ who picks up the burden on our behalf. His is the only complete forgiveness. All our attempts fall short. '*O Lamb of God, that takest away the sins of the world, grant us thy peace*,' we pray in the Eucharist as we approach the Sacrament of Christ's Body and Blood. And one of those sins is our failure to forgive. A meditation upon the Cross reminds us who it is that bears the consequence of that failure.

Sure, *Dieu nous pardonnera*, but at a cost.

DON'T BLAME GOD FOR THE WEATHER

To blame God for the disasters of flood, quake, drought and famine is nothing new. And so when two bishops of the Church of England were reported (actually, in one case, entirely misreported, and in the other partially so) as having said that the floods in July (2007) were divine punishment for the sins of society, it was no surprise. Even so, the idea that God inflicts havoc upon the lives of one part of the population in order to punish the sins of another, is silly by any standard of belief, Christian or otherwise.

Recruiting divine support for one's own point of view in order to scare the opposition is as old as the Trojan War. And what an unseemly mess *that* was. But at least the ancient Greeks had the excuse of their pagan religion; that's to say, with all those shenanigans on Mount Olympus, they were bound to have low expectations of divine conduct. Christians have no such excuse. Even the slightest knowledge of Jesus's life and teaching must exclude the possibility of believing in a God who could inflict such selective, unjust, and, let's face it, inefficient penalties.

Yet there persists the desire to ascribe natural disasters to the wrath of God. One of the greatest disasters to hit Europe happened in 1755, when Lisbon was destroyed by earthquake, fire and flood. The tragedy provoked consternation in the drawing rooms of Europe. The King of France put aside his mistress. She, not wishing to be outdone, put aside her rouge. In England, gentlemen at White's abandoned their cards. At the Haymarket Theatre a masquerade was cancelled. A Day of National Fast was proclaimed. John Wesley thundered against the rich. It was all their fault, he said. 'It comes!' he declaimed,

'It comes! The roof trembles! The beams crack! The ground rocks to and fro... Wealthy fool, where is now thy golden god?' Stirring stuff, indeed.

Not everyone was caught up in the moral panic. One preacher confided to his congregation that he would not comment upon the catastrophe. 'A presumptuous forwardness in pronouncing on extraordinary events,' he said, 'we leave to raving monks and Methodists.' (to which we might add bishops). He had a point, though I doubt that anyone today would be quite so rude.

Let the Bible have the last word.

My thoughts are not your thoughts, neither are your ways my ways, saith the Lord. For as the heavens are higher than the earth, so are my ways than your ways, and my thoughts than your thoughts.

(Isaiah 55: 8,9).

So who are we to ascribe bad weather to divine wrath?

DOVER BEACH

'*Come to the window*', wrote Matthew Arnold in his poem 'Dover Beach',

> *The sea is calm tonight, the tide is full   Listen! you hear the*
> *grating roar*
> *Of pebbles which the waves draw back, and fling,*
> *At their return, up the high strand,*
> *Begin, and cease, and then again begin,*
> *With tremulous cadence slow, and bring*
> *The eternal note of sadness in.*
>
> *The Sea of Faith*
> *Was once, too, at the full, and round earth's shore*
> *Lay like the folds of a bright girdle furled.*
> *But now I only hear*
> *Its melancholy, long, withdrawing roar,*
> *Retreating, to the breath*
> *Of the night-wind, down the vast edges drear*
> *And naked shingles of the world.*

His words haunt the mind and capture the desolation of a world that has lost its faith. Once the sea of faith had been 'at the full', but now the tide was going out. He wrote those words in 1867. Were they true then? Are they true now? Most people over the age of forty take a gloomy view of life, though few can put it so well as Matthew Arnold. But was he right, and are people right now, a century and a half later, to dismiss faith as a private enterprise of only marginal significance in the public life of a modern state?

Well, for all its beauty Matthew Arnold's poem was wrong, and for all its huffing and puffing the National Secular Society is out of step with the overwhelming majority of our fellow citizens. Faith, whether Christian or otherwise, is widely held in modern Britain to be an important ingredient in society and has a public role. It cannot be dismissed as the private hobby of a few eccentrics.

How people express that faith, whether in the traditional formularies of church, synagogue, mosque and temple, or in informal, provisional and free-wheeling groupings, is another matter. Mistrust and impatience with formal religion is a widespread phenomenon and challenges all faiths. But this sort of questioning attitude should not necessarily be seen as a loss of faith. We are so often being told that church attendance is dwindling, and national statistics do seem to support the view that organised religion is in terminal decline. But is it? Three random statistics suggest it is not all gloom and doom. During the Pope's visit in 2010, 80,000 people (young and old) gathered in Hyde Park to celebrate their faith; in the past ten years attendance at worship in English cathedrals rose by twenty-four per cent; in a picture of the interior of Withyham Church on Christmas Eve 1848, there are only four people visible in the congregation; on Christmas Eve 2009 there were 130. Make of that what you will. Raw statistics can be made to prove anything!

ENGLISH TRANSLATIONS OF THE BIBLE

2011 was the fourth centenary of the publication, in 1611, of the Authorised Version of the Bible, now known as the King James Version. By command of King James I, a committee of fifty-four scholars, working in six teams, two each at Westminster, Oxford and Cambridge, spent about seven years translating the scriptures from the original Hebrew and Greek. They had before them the work of previous translators. Here are two examples of earlier versions of the opening verses of the Book of Genesis. You can compare them with 1611 version.

Wyclif c1380

In the bigynnyng God made of nouyt heuene and erthe. Forsothe the erthe was idel and voide, and derknessis weren on the face of depthe; and the Spiryt of the Lord was borun on the watris. And God seide, Liyt be maad, and liyt was maad.

Tyndale c1525

In the begynnynge God created heaven and erth. The erth was voyde and emptie and darcknesse was vpon the depe and the spirite of god moved vpon the water. Than God sayd: let there be lyghte and there was lyghte.

King James Version 1611

In the beginning God created the heaven and the earth. And the earth was without form, and void; and darkness was upon the face of the deep. And the Spirit of God moved upon the face of the waters. And God said, Let there be light: and there was light.

Although Christianity had been the predominant religion in our country since the sixth century, the only authorised version of the Bible until the sixteenth century had been in Latin. Not a lot of help to the average man or woman in the pew, you might think. The official view was that Latin was the top language, and besides, it was well understood by the clergy. They seemed to have forgotten that Jesus spoke Aramaic and St Paul spoke and wrote Greek, but there we are. Ecclesiastical authority can sometimes be astonishingly obtuse.

William Knighton, a chronicler writing in 1390, deplored the Wycliffite translation of the Bible. He described it as a translation from 'the language of angels into the language of Angles'. Knighton was not the first to make that pun. But he went further. He regretted that the English translation could now be heard and understood by the uneducated and by women.

The argument about which is God's language re-appears from time to time, and often in the most surprising places. Milton, although himself a Latinist, believed that English was the favoured tongue: 'When God speaks, he speaks first to Englishmen.' Now, *there's* a thought.

FLORENCE NIGHTINGALE WAS
BORED TO DESPERATION

During her life Florence Nightingale was revered almost as a saint. The image of 'The Lady with the Lamp' took its place in the nation's gallery of icons. But she very nearly did not make it. In those days the pressures against a woman doing anything other than sit at home were immense. Of course, it was entirely possible to do a great deal within that sphere, but for many women it was a claustrophobic restriction.

Florence Nightingale was a sociable, funny, lively, attractive, highly intelligent, well-connected young woman, and not without her suitors. She glittered and danced and played her part in London's ballrooms and fashionable drawing rooms. In the country life was less exciting. 'What have I done this fortnight?' she wrote in July 1846. 'I have read *The Daughter at Home* to Father and two chapters of Macintosh; a volume of *Sybil* to Mamma. Learnt seven new tunes by heart. Written various letters. Ridden with Papa. Paid eight visits. Done Company. And that is all'. She was bored. In her words, 'bored to desperation'. She was 26 years old.

She was not only bored. Unknown to the world, which saw only an agreeable and accomplished young woman, she was racked with guilt, tormented by the knowledge that she was capable of so much more, and that God was calling her to a higher purpose. The struggle against her family's opposition to follow that calling would have broken most daughters. It nearly broke her. 'I cannot live', she wrote in a private note, 'Forgive me, O Lord, and let me die.' Added to this, she suffered from a dark, disabling sense of her own sinfulness. Sheer strength of will carried her through, but at what a cost.

To achieve what she believed was her purpose in life, she had to give up so much. Friendship, she said, could be a distraction. 'Dearest, it is well that we should not see too much of each other,' she wrote to a close friend, 'Farewell, my beloved one.' And in a private note she wrote, 'O God, no more love. No more marriage, O God.'

By an act of will, she became what in that culture she needed to be: a single-minded, domineering, wilful, manipulative martinet, feared by every person in the land save one, and that was Queen Victoria. She would have got nowhere by being gentle and kind.

It is hard to believe that so many generations of women were held back, compelled to submit or bravely to strive, and in doing so become oddities in the eyes of their contemporaries. When, in 1980, the Church drew up a list of modern worthies to be commemorated in her calendar, the twenty names included only one woman. Why such disparity? 'Because,' came the answer, 'conduct which was regarded as sanctity in men was regarded as insanity in women.' Well, we have moved on a bit since then, but we still have a way to go.

FORAGING AMONG THE MANUSCRIPTS

A pastedown is part of the binding of a book. It is the outer leaf of an endpaper that is glued down to the inside of the hard covers and is an essential part of the book's structure. During Tudor times many college and cathedral libraries were casting out their medieval texts, and replacing them with works of the New Learning. The market for discarded parchment, a valuable commodity, was flooded with manuscripts from college libraries and from the plundered monasteries. These ancient texts, including service books and choir music, were cut into strips and put to good use in the binding of new works.

Anthony à Wood, the seventeenth century antiquarian of Oxford, recorded that older members of his college, Merton, still remembered how in the previous century medieval manuscripts from their library had been hauled away in cartloads to the binders' workshops. Some of them returned to the college as fragments in the binding of new acquisitions. A parchment leaf used as a wrapper of the college Steward's Account Book of 1596 had been cut from Peter of Cornwall's *Pantheologia* of 1189, a vast compendium of biblical texts, the original purpose of which was to provide an aid to preachers. It now served a more practical purpose.

John Aubrey, a friend of Wood's and an antiquarian too, wrote that at the Dissolution of the monasteries the monks' manuscripts 'went flying around like butterflies through the air. A hundred years later, it seems to me that they are still on the wing. I would net them if I could. It hurts my eyes and heart to see fragile painted pages used to line pastry dishes, to bung up bottles, to cover school books or make templates beneath a tailor's scissors.'

And yet four centuries later we must be grateful to the
bookbinders, if not to the cooks and tailors, for unwittingly
preserving enough fragments to give tantalising glimpses of a
vanished world.

Aubrey, who spent so much time recording the details of his
contemporaries' lives, left only a few autobiographical notes,
which he said, might 'be interponed as a sheet of waste-paper
in the binding of a book.' He was a master of self-deprecation.

And what of our own slender biographies? When we have
gone, will those fragile painted pages of our brief lives flutter
like butterflies in the memories of our friends and children?
Perhaps we dare not hope for that. A worthier end of our life's
work might be to serve, unobserved and unrewarded, as lining
for a pastry dish, to bung a bottle or two, to cover a school
book or make a template for a tailor's scissors.

FRESHERS' WEEK

Some of you have just said goodbye to your sons and daughters as they headed off to university for the start of a new life. You may have reflected, as you drove away from the campus with an empty car, that parting is such sweet sorrow. Well, up to a point. You will soon learn that they will return. Oh, yes, they will come back all right, again and again and again. They still need you.

This is what a student, Paul Behain, wrote to his widowed mother in Nuremberg in 1574:

> *'Dear Mother... I have used the money from the sale of my horse to have the simplest coarse green clothing made for myself – a doublet with modest trim, pleatless hose and hooded coat. Lest you think things are cheap here, all this has cost me approximately 17 or 18 crowns, even though it was as plain and simple as it could be. I could not have been more amazed when I saw the bill than you will be when I send it to you.'*

You may ask what the boy did with the money from the horse, if his tailor's bill remained unpaid. Ah, well, life can be sweet at eighteen, can it not? And devilish expensive. But, then, what's a parent for if not to pick up the tab?

Another worry you may face is your children's sudden change of career choice. Just as you had planned for your daughter a safe career in law, she tells you that she wants to go on the stage. Mr and Mrs Zebedee must have wondered what their sons, James and John, were doing when one day they threw up their secure future in the family business to go after that young preacher from Nazareth.

Their story, like so much in the Gospel narrative, is tantalisingly sketchy. However, it does give us just enough detail to glimpse the support given by their families to those young men, including the one from Nazareth, as they followed the dream which led them to Jerusalem and the redemption of the human race. The women who provided for them while they were on the road *'out of their resources'* (Luke 8: 1-3) – who were they, if not their mothers, aunts and older sisters?

A cynic might snort at the comparison. Young Paul Behain's tailor's bill can in no way be likened to the cost to their parents of the disciples' vocation. But who knows? The feckless youth with his green doublet and hose might have grown up to be like his late father – a successful merchant and worthy citizen of Nuremberg. The panache and sheer cheek of his letter boded well for his future. His mother paid the bill, but had no way of knowing how he would turn out.

He may have come good, or he may have gone to the bad and grown up a wastrel, a charming rogue, a prodigal son – but, one hopes, a son with a patient and forgiving parent like the father in the parable.

GROCERS AND SAINTS

Some while ago it was announced in the situations vacant column of the *Church Times* that the Worshipful Company of Grocers was wishing to appoint a clergyman as incumbent of a well-known city church.

Now you may be surprised – you may even be shocked – that the purveyors of pickles and preserves should possess the right to appoint a clergyman to his benefice. It puts Fortnum & Mason into quite a new light.

But you should not be surprised, and you should certainly not be offended. There has always been in our country a rather blurred line between the sacred and the secular. After all, it was not all that long ago – only a century and a half – that the Dean and Chapter of York owned a public house in that city known as 'The Old Rackett'.

We should not worry that grocers are involved in church appointments. On the contrary, we should start to worry when grocers, and, for that matter, butchers, bakers and candlestick makers, cease to be involved in church affairs.

When trade separates itself from religion, both are impoverished. It is the recognition that ecclesiastical, social, commercial and political elements of our national life interlock which underlies what we mean by an Established Church.

Now, of course, the establishment creaks in some of its joints. It is full of archaic oddities which once made sense, but have now lost their meaning and which, like the nosegay carried by the Queen at the Royal Maundy to ward off the smell of the poor, are now of more ornament than use.

There is another reason why the sight of grocers in search of a parson is more fitting than might at first appear.

If you go back to your copy of Edward Gibbon's *Decline and Fall of the Roman Empire* you will find his account of St George. He identifies our national saint with one George of Cappadocia, who, having been in trade in a small way, had the good fortune to secure an exclusive contract to supply bacon to the imperial army. After that, George never looked back.

Gibbon's version may or may not be historically correct, but it does reveal our national saint in a more plausible light. Instead of a valiant knight and dragon killer, we are presented with the spectacle of a shrewd grocer. How suitable for a nation of shop-keepers.

It is no bad thing to be reminded that the Church has to deploy the talents of a thrifty shopkeeper as well as the showy image of a knight on horseback. It is, after all, no good galloping around the world looking for dragons to slay, if you do not have an efficient organisation to sustain you with the necessary provisions for your mission.

A DISSENTER'S HAIL MARY

You bore him, fed him, clothed him, led him,
you carried him, suckled him, sang him to sleep.
You nursed him, enfolded him, encouraged him, scolded him,
you suffered him, moved him to laugh (and to weep).
You were the chosen one, you were the maiden.
He was yours before he was ours.
With your flesh the Word was laden,
Seed of eternity, Hope of the years.
For your obedience, your faith and your firmness,
for your humility, tenderness, grace,
sinners salute you, presume to say 'Thank you',
who love him and serve him, but had not your place.

(James Badcock)

Mary should be honoured in our prayers. She is our sister-in-faith; too young to be our mother, although we call her 'Mother of God'. And there's our difficulty. As children of the Reformation, we find that her titles (Mother of God; Queen of heaven) get in the way.

At the Reformation our ancestors rejected the cult of Mary, but their rejection, fuelled by the New Learning at the universities, was too harsh. Country people, brought up to honour Mary in their parish church with candles and images as a focus for their prayer, were bewildered when their beloved statues were smashed and their devotions scorned by the clever-clogs from town.

Richard Graye was rector of Withyham during those turbulent years. One source records that he was instituted rector in 1540 (not 1576 as indicated on our rectors' board

in church) and held the living through four Tudor reigns, at a time when the church swung backwards and forwards between Rome, Geneva and Canterbury. What could he and his parishioners do as church officialdom removed, then replaced, and finally destroyed the altar and its ornaments in Withyham church's north aisle, the one they called 'the Lady aisle' in honour of Mary? His will shows him as a conscientious priest and pastor.

It is not likely that he and his parishioners ceased to honour Mary in their prayers, whatever the official view might be. The 'Hail Mary,' like the 'Our Father', was a prayer they learnt in the vernacular at their mother's knee; it was deeply rooted in their souls. They knew it in English, not in Latin like the Mass, and so it took two generations at least for the 'Hail Mary' to drop out of the memory and prayers of Englishmen and women. To our great loss.

March 25th, Lady Day, commemorates the Annunciation when the angel Gabriel first spoke the words *Hail Mary, full of grace, the Lord is with thee,* which were then amplified by those of Mary's cousin Elizabeth, *Blessed art thou among women, blessed is the fruit of thy womb, Jesus.*

JOHN THE BAPTIST HAD NO SMALL TALK

On Jordan's bank the Baptist's cry
Announces that the Lord is nigh.

John the Baptist had no small talk. Or so it seems. That uncomfortable, abrasive, intimidating figure, whom we admire, but would not care to meet, saved his breath for sterner stuff.

If you were to ask him round to your place ('Just a few of us – kitchen supper'), or invite him to one of your little drinks parties ('Smart casual') he would not turn up. Chances are he would not even reply to your invitation. The niceties of social convention do not figure prominently on Jordan's Bank,

On the other hand, if you were to invite his cousin, Jesus of Nazareth, the chances are that he *would* turn up, and that he would enjoy your hospitality.

Why such a contrast between the two cousins: the prophet who set his face against society, and the Son of God who seemed to be compliant with its conventions? Jesus himself drew attention to this distinction. *'John came,'* he said, *'Neither eating nor drinking, and they say, He hath a devil; the Son of Man came eating and drinking, and they say, Behold a man gluttonous and a wine-bibber, a friend of tax-collectors and sinners.'*

These may at first sight be words of comfort to you and me.

'Ah, yes,' we murmur as we help ourselves to another *mignon morceau,* 'How well he knows our needs. What was that he said? *The Son of Man came not to call the righteous, but sinners,'* we murmur, and tilt the decanter judiciously to our glass.

But have we read the text correctly? Go back to it and we

will see that the sinners with whom Jesus sat down to eat – the ones he called his friends – left the table at the end of the meal challenged by the encounter. Sharing supper with him was not always a comfortable experience. Conviviality gave way to repentance.

Zacchaeus, the swindling tax-collector of Jericho, found salvation unexpectedly at lunch in the presence of the uninvited guest from Nazareth (Luke 19: 1-10). Matthew, called Levi, another tax-collector, responded to Jesus's call by inviting him to a dinner party, and it was at that dinner that his guest spoke those words, *'The Son of Man came not to call the righteous, but sinners'* (Luke 5:27-32). For Matthew, it was the beginning of a journey that would lead to the Last Supper in the upper room, and eventually to his martyrdom in a distant land.

Repentance may come to us in the wilderness, or it may steal up on us at a dinner party, or it may catch us unawares as we savour a second glass of that excellent dry sherry. But it's never going to be easy.

A JOLLY GOOD TUNE

One morning, as she was strolling on the terrace of Windsor Castle, Queen Victoria was struck by the tune a workman was whistling. She sent to enquire the name of the song. '"Oh, wont you take me where the booze is cheap", Ma'am', she was told. 'Ah, yes', she said, and thanked the footman for the information.

Noel Coward, head tilted back, cigarette poised, looked across the balcony at Gertrude Lawrence, and, as the sounds of the hotel orchestra drifted up to them, he muttered through clenched teeth, 'Strange how potent cheap music is'.

A good tune breaks down the highest barriers, softens the hardest heart. It was, after all, the tune of a popular carol which brought the German and the British soldiers out of their trenches to shake hands in No Man's Land during a lull in the fighting on Christmas Eve 1914. And in the Second World War, it was the haunting melody of 'Lily Marlene' broadcast nightly on German radio in North Africa to which the British troops as well as German listened, whistled, sang.

I heard once – probably on the radio – an eminent classical musician (and I wish I could remember who) saying that one of the greatest songs to be written in the twentieth century was in his opinion 'Smoke gets in your eyes'... or was it 'A nightingale sang in Berkeley Square'? Whichever, the point is the same.

Another distinguished composer – and this one's name I *can* recall; it was Arthur Sullivan – claimed that the most satisfying hymn tune was the Old Hundredth (All people that on earth do dwell*)*. Its stately measure may be too solemn for the taste of most, but, brought to this country from Geneva by returning protestant exiles at the beginning of Queen Elizabeth I's reign, it has been part of the national repertoire ever since.

Given the potency of a good tune, it is no wonder that some of our best loved hymns are sung to what began as the melodies of popular songs. One of our greatest is derived from a galliard which in an earlier form is set to the carol 'Remember, O thou man'. A later version was that great tankard-thumping ale-house shout which got itself hitched sometime during the reign of George II to the no less thundering words, 'God save great George our King'. It was the world's first National Anthem, and it remains the best.

More surprising is the origin of Helmsley, the tune of that fine Advent hymn, 'Lo, he comes with clouds descending'. It began life as 'Miss Catley's Hornpipe', a robust and saucy ballad, popular with eighteenth century audiences in Vauxhall Gardens. What matter? The magic of a good tune is one of the loveliest features of God's creation, and so why should we hesitate to sing it, whatever its provenance, to his praise and glory?

KEEP ME, O LORD, AS THE APPLE OF AN EYE

Keep me, O Lord, as the apple of an eye;
Hide me under the shadow of thy wings.
Compline (BCP 1928) and Night Prayer (CW 2005)

'The apple of an eye: a symbol of that which is most cherished,' declares the Oxford English Dictionary in its stern, matter-of-fact way, but there is no disguising the beauty of this most lovely of phrases. Moses used it in his song of delight, celebrating the Lord, who *saved Jacob from the howling wilderness, guarding him as the apple of his eye and covering him beneath the shadow of his wings* (Deuteronomy 32:10). The Psalmist sang the same words of comfort (psalm 17:8). Centuries later they found their way into the monastic office of compline, revived for Anglicans in the *Cuddesdon Office Book* (19th c), then by the 1928 revision of the *Book of Common Prayer*, and now by Common Worship under the title *Night Prayer*

As a sixth-former I found myself, rather to my surprise, attending compline one evening in the school chapel at Lancing. I knew that some of the more pious boys would disappear at 9.00 pm on Fridays in Lent. I went along out of curiosity, not expecting much.

The Lord Almighty grant us a quiet night and a perfect end... Whoso dwelleth under the defence of the most high shall abide under the shadow the Almighty... Keep me, O Lord, as the apple an eye, hide me under the shadow thy wings

The quiet reflective tone struck me; so different from what I was accustomed to in chapel. Here were words of deep refreshment. Amazing stuff! It was not a Damascus Road experience, and it certainly did not happen all at once, but it was a beginning (there were to be many others).

There was more than just bland re-assurance. There was something darker too: a hint of menace to set in high relief the words of comfort. *Be sober, be vigilant, because your adversary the devil, as a roaring lion, walketh about, seeking whom he may devour; whom resist steadfast in the faith.* What eighteen-year-old does not know the devil within or has not sensed his or her own howling wilderness? *Hide me under the shadow of thy wings.*

Then there was that rare use of the first person singular. Not *keep us,* but *keep me as the apple of an eye.* Most of our public praying is in the plural, as you would expect it to be in common prayer, but now, at bedtime, we revert to our private childhood moment when we were tucked up by mother. *Sweet dreams, darling, sleep well.* Just her and me, the apple of her eye. Did the monks, I wonder, find solace in that memory, and see in it a foreshadowing of God, as they entered the 'greater silence', and filed off down a draughty cloister to a bleak dormitory? Did it redress the relentlessly corporate nature of community life?

Before the ending of the day Creator of the world we pray. Just in case I forget, just in case I am carried away by my private moment with God, the words of the compline hymn bring me back in line. And there is the miracle: that the one who cherishes each of us as the apple of his eye, the one who calls us each his darling, is the God of all creation, the Love that moves the sun and stars.

LOOKING BACK

'No one who sets his hand to the plough and keeps looking back is fit for the Kingdom of God.'

(Luke 9:62)

Those are hard words. Particularly hard when you consider to whom they were spoken. The would-be disciple of Jesus had said, *'I will follow you, but first let me say good-bye to my people at home.'* Jesus was not impressed. And the man was left behind on the road looking wistfully at the leader whom he lacked the courage to follow.

He must have stood there for a moment, torn between the impossible claims of Jesus, and the gentler demands of life. Of course, the request to be allowed to say good-bye to his family was only an excuse; the latest in a series of excuses to delay his decision. 'Yes, Lord, I'll follow you… in time.'

We are skilful in our excuses. There is no end to our resourcefulness in putting off the decision which we know that in the end we will have to make. We play with religion to gratify our hearts, but we are cautious lest our dalliance become too serious.

Our coyness with Christ would be no crime were we still with him in Galilee. But now, on the road to Jerusalem, with his face set resolutely towards Calvary, we have neither world enough nor time to go on flirting with his love.

A young man I knew sought the advice of an old priest. The room they sat in, which was not far from Westminster Abbey, was sparsely furnished. A prie-dieu for him; a wooden chair for the priest; a large uncompromising crucifix upon the wall. Having made confession of all his wretched inadequacies and

failures, the young man waited for words of advice, comfort and absolution from the priest. But when the words came, they were as hard as nails, as stark as the cross. 'No one who sets his hand to the plough and keeps looking back is fit for the Kingdom of God.'

The young man's re-action was one of resentment. He had asked of the priest bread and had received a stone. Or so it seemed. 'Silly old fool', he thought, as he stepped into the sunshine of a summer's day. 'What can that old fossil, locked away in his gloomy religion, know about the joys and temptations of this beautiful world?' And walking through St James's Park, loveliest of London's royal gardens, he tried to shake off the memory of those words, and catch the carefree mood of the crowd.

He nearly succeeded. But not quite. Because he found that ever after in the careless sunlit capital of his heart there remained that private room with its crucifix and hard unyielding message.

MARTYRS: ANCIENT & MODERN

What comes to mind when you hear the word 'Martyr'? A Christian being thrown to the lions in ancient Rome? Someone being burnt at the stake by the Tudors? But martyrdom is still with us. According to one website the number of Christians killed for their faith in 2016 was 90,000. The number is probably exaggerated, but there is no doubt that faith-related torture and murder are features of our contemporary world.

Of course, the statistics are unclear (as ever), and include many instances of tribal, ethnic or political, but not religious, persecution. To take an example close to home: if a man is killed in the course of a street fight between Muslims and Christians in, let's say, London or Bradford, would you say he was a martyr? Probably not. Although difference of faith might have been an issue, it was only incidental to the fight. You would not say he had died for Christ or for Mahomet. The same was certainly true of all those tragic deaths during the 'troubles' in Northern Ireland: the victims may have been brave, or unlucky, or, in some cases, foolish. They may have put themselves at risk in the course of duty, or they may have been the unwilling casualties of violence. I doubt if any of them was motivated by a desire to witness to Christ, although they may have been devout Christians, as some surely were.

The tribal hatred which poisons so many nations (our own included) often wears a religious mask because the ancient boundaries of ethnic or political allegiance coincide with those of faith or denomination. When the Christian Bosnian Serbs murdered 8,000 Muslim Bosnian men and boys at Srebrenica in 1995, and 'ethnically cleansed' 25,000 others in the region, it was a racist, not a religious crime; one of unimaginable horror, but the victims were victims of hate, they were not martyrs.

Janani Luwum, Archbishop of Uganda, spoke out against the wicked tyranny of President Amin. He did so fully knowing what would happen. It did happen. He disappeared, murdered by the command, possibly even by the hand of Amin. Janani Luwum was a martyr, as was Father Maximilian Kolbe, a polish priest imprisoned in Auschwitz who offered to take the place of a fellow prisoner sentenced to death. There have been many others in our lifetime.

What would I do if I was in Luwum or Kolbe's shoes? Or in the place of Hugh Latimer and Nicholas Ridley, burnt at the stake in 1555 (their anniversaries fall on 16th October). It is not a question I care to ponder, as I am sure I would keep my head down and slink off into the shadows, hoping not to be seen. What would you do? And yet... and yet... there have been so many men and women, not specially brave, who, when faced with torture have been given by God a courage and strength they never knew they had in them. They died defiantly. 'Be of good comfort Master Ridley, and play the man' said Latimer to his fellow martyr as the fires were lit, 'We shall this day light such a candle by God's grace in England, as, I trust, shall never be put out.'

MIND, HEART AND WILL:
THE BALANCED PRAYER

*Eternal God, who art the light of the minds that know thee,
the joy of the hearts that love thee, and the strength of the wills
that serve thee: Grant us so to know thee that we may truly
love thee, and so to love thee that we may fully serve thee,
whom to serve is perfect freedom. Amen.*

(After St. Augustine AD 396-430)

This prayer has for centuries been prayed in countless languages
throughout the world. It is cast in the form of a collect, whose
compact simplicity allows complex theological truths to be
easily memorised and repeated, and by repetition to become
not only a vehicle for Christian devotion, but its pattern.

The classical tradition of Christian spirituality holds the
three elements of our personality in balance: Mind, Heart
and Will. Too much mind, and our faith becomes formal;
too much emotion, and it dissolves into sentiment; too much
determination, and it becomes a striving after achievement,
leading to spiritual arrogance and, in the face of failure, to
despair.

The Church of England in its different moods has
sometimes displayed the dangers of imbalance. Once it was
dry and stuffy and deeply boring: a duty to attend, but an
impossibility to enjoy. Then in the glory days of the 1950s
when numbers were up and success was visible and parish
churches spawned countless organisations by which to convert
society, she became arrogant and over-concerned about her
own achievements. Busy, busy, busy: too much activity and
not enough reflection.

Then, when the bubble of success went pop and people stopped coming to church, she was tempted to withdraw into herself. She went a little mad, indulging in eccentric practices, waving her arms about in the sure belief that she was saved, and thereby frightening away many of her fringe members who were not sure if they were saved, and even if they were, did not entirely want to be if it meant singing twaddle and waving their arms – and that was a shame because the strength of the C of E is in her fringe. 'Alleluia! Alleluia!' we learnt to sing, with too much heart and very little brain.

What we need in life and worship is the balance of St Augustine's prayer. We must start by engaging our minds in thinking about the glory of God as revealed in the world and as learnt from the life and teaching of Christ. That is the first movement: it lays the foundation for the next, which is to turn from this cerebral exercise to a response of the heart in wonder, penitence, praise and thanks. That is the second movement, but it cannot stop there, for we are then propelled towards the third movement: an engagement of the will to re-align our lives, and to go on doing so even when emotional enthusiasm runs dry. One movement leads to another; each feeds and is fed by the other.

Our Church, both national and local, and also our personal faith, must ever be checked and measured against the pattern of this prayer.

MOORHENS AND MORTALITY

There is a pond I know where moorhens nest. Each year the resident pair produces a second clutch, only one of their first brood having survived to adolescence. The second brood of six chicks have a lovely time swimming around the pond and scampering about on the lily pads under the watchful eye of their parents. What prettier sight can you find?

But nature is less kind than we would have her be. Built into her design is the intention that only two or three of the chicks should survive. Else in four generations our ponds and water meadows would be overrun by hordes of hungry moorhens. Beneath the smiling surface of the pond on which those little chicks delight to play, nature has placed a predatory pike. From time to time he reaches up to snatch and gobble. Alarmed, his victims scurry to the bank, unaware of the waiting fox.

You and I, as we sip our iced drinks beneath the sunshade and muse upon these things, are shocked that nature should be so cruel; that there should be so much violence in her economy. Then we see a wasp crawling menacingly towards our bare arm; without a second's thought we swat the creature dead. We are partial in our sympathies. We criticise nature's haphazard morality and require her to be kind to moorhen chicks and harvest mice, but we are not too bothered about the survival of wasps and slugs, ants and flies, all of which we happily destroy.

Our trouble is this: we see only half the picture. I am as selective in my view of nature as the next man. I love the sight of a hawk soaring, hovering and plummeting, but I blench at the purpose of all that superb mastery of the sky: the hooked beak tearing at the warm flesh of its still living prey.

Where does God enter the picture? I suppose that you might take the view that the Creator has made a bit of a hash of things. Just look at the cuckoo, programmed to be a home-wrecker. Not very nice. Either creation is flawed, in which case the Creator has bungled. Or those things we consider flaws, are not so at all, but, are, in the longer perspective, essential parts of a larger, more wonderful mechanism than we can comprehend.

'*But the last enemy is death*', St Paul said. Ah, yes, Death, the biggest flaw of all. The contradiction of nature's benevolence. We pour ourselves another glass and shift uneasily on the sun-lounger. Beneath the smiling surface of the pond the pike awaits its turn.

Gloomy? Morbid? Not really. Not if you accept the fact that mortality (and her sisters grief and pain), far from being intruders, are themselves part of the scene, part of the plan. God in Christ enters the scene, stands alongside, enjoys, endures, and dies with us. And since his rising from the grave, every part of his creation is edged in flame, and raised to glory.

Meanwhile,

'*Golden lads and girls all must*
As chimney sweepers come to dust.'

Our pleasures on this earth must always be provisional and tinged with melancholy. We will know when we have got to heaven: it will be when we can enjoy that second drink without foreboding, confident that we are loved, and knowing at last that we really have nothing to fear.

PILLAR OR BUTTRESS?

'While I cannot be regarded as a pillar of the church, I must be regarded as a buttress, because I support it from the outside.' so said Lord Melbourne, Queen Victoria's first Prime Minister.

He was one of our more likeable prime ministers. He refused to take himself or his office too seriously. 'Damn it all, another bishop dead? I verily believe they die to vex me,' he muttered as he faced the task of filling a vacant see.

What he said was quite true (about being a buttress, that is – not sure about the bishops). He was one of those genial people, honourable and well disposed towards their fellow human beings, who conceal their goodness and generosity beneath a cloak of irony. Not a bad description, you might say, of all that is best in the English character.

Many of us – most of us – no, *all* of us (let's not be pernickety), all of us fit that profile like a glove, but, of course, being the modest people that we are, we would be the last to say so. Genial, generous, honourable, tolerant... *like a glove,* to be sure.

But are we pillars or buttresses? Well, that is for each of us to judge. The job of a parish priest is to make sure that in our church we have plenty of both! Of course, the clergy would dearly love all the buttresses to become pillars, but they know that's not going to happen, for all sorts of reasons. (Yes, I know, I know... remove all the buttresses and the walls would fall out).

The Church of England has a low threshold and a large porch. That is to say, she should be easily accessible. She should allow people to slip in without fuss, to hover uncertainly in the doorway if necessary, perhaps to step back outside without guilt or recrimination – but she hopes they will come in and stay.

The Parish Church exists for the whole community, not for her own membership. That is why we use the title 'Church of England'. The boundaries of her membership are deliberately blurred, her disciplines unobtrusive. Of course, that makes her look vague, weak and woolly, but it is her vocation. Each denomination (RC, Orthodox, Free Church, Pentecostalist etc.) has its own particular role within the universal Church of God. Some have a vocation to make strict institutional demands upon their members – to raise the threshold and clarify the boundaries – but that is not ours.

Ours is to keep open house.

PRAYER: THE DAILY TOOTHBRUSH

I heard of a man, an academic theologian, so caught up in his thoughts that he had little time to consider the trivia of daily life. Rising in the morning, shaving, brushing his teeth, dressing, tying his shoe laces, eating, drinking: such things were distractions from the purpose of his solitary life. To manage them he adopted, as most of us do, a routine by which these commonplace actions could be performed unconsciously, each triggering the next. The toothbrush, the flannel, the razor, the towel were just the beginning of a sequence of automatic manoeuvres which extended via the kettle, the coffee, the car, the commute, lectures, meetings, tutorials and so on, through the waking hours of day until their conclusion was reached at night via the kettle, the nightcap, the hot water bottle, the toothbrush, prayer and sleep.

By such a strategy he claimed to set his mind free to consider the deeper things of life. All the while that he performed 'the trivial round, the common task', attending to them with the barest minimum of mental and emotional energy, the vast engine of his mind turned ceaselessly and silently through the endless revolutions of abstract thought. He was, was he not, the greatest living expert on the Chalcedonian Definition. His paper on the Eutychian heresy delivered at a recent international symposium on Patristics in the University of Uppsala was said to be the last word on that fraught and well-worn topic.

Then, one morning something went wrong.

Chancing to go upstairs to the bathroom to remove a speck from his eye (he had finished breakfast and was about to go to work), he caught sight of his toothbrush. At the time he was thinking about the second epistle of St Cyril. The motor of routine kicked in. Unconsciously his hand picked up the brush, and cleaned his teeth. Slowly he undressed, put on his pyjamas, folded only an hour before, said his prayers and went to bed. Outside his house the twentieth century went roaring past along the Woodstock Road, and all the while inside his head the vast and silent engine of his mind went round and round and round and round.

We live on several levels of reality, you and I. The trick is not to lose touch with any of them; not to disconnect the trivial from the serious, the routine from the rare. Each feeds the other. Prayer, that often forgotten little bit of business (a hurried 'Our Father' as one wakes; a brief committal into God's safe keeping as one lies down to sleep), inhabits the upper level of the mind, keeping company with toothbrush and flannel, but its repeated utterance connects with the deepest level of the soul which all the while, ceaselessly and silently, unfolds beneath the gentle influence of the Creator's forgiving love.

PRAYER CANDLES

Suddenly there are candles everywhere. No longer to lighten our path; electricity does that well enough. Candlelight, that ancient invention, has found so many new uses: on the dinner table to celebrate a feast; on the cake to mark an anniversary; in the alcove to add lustre to a dark corner; on the roadside to mourn a death; and gathering in multitudes on the steps of public buildings to voice a silent protest or proclaim a jubilee.

If you are going to the continent this summer for your holiday, you may find yourself visiting a great cathedral – say, Chartres or Cologne or Palermo – or you may chance upon the cool shade of an unremarkable parish church, and make an unscheduled visit to escape the blistering glare of the mid-day sun. There you will probably see, once you have got used to the dark, a cluster of candles burning on a stand in one of the chapels. Like a growing number of tourists you may be moved to drop a coin in the box and light a candle and then – then what? *'Je ne sais pas comment prier'*, says a notice next to the candle-stand in Sens Cathedral –

> *'I do not know how to pray. I do not know what to say.*
> *I do not have much time. This candle is something of what*
> *I have.*
> *Something of my time, something of myself that I leave*
> *Before the Lord. This light that shines is my prayer.'*

You might remember someone you know back home who is in trouble, sorrow, need or sickness, and let the candle burn for them. And, later, don't be shy to tell them. Gestures of affection are never wasted.

Or you might just be silent, and reflect with T S Eliot when you light that small candle that you are standing where others have prayed and in a place –

where prayer is valid. And prayer is more
than an order of words, the conscious occupation
of the praying mind, or the sound of the voice praying.

Wherever and however you spend your summer holiday, may you find refreshment and recreation of body, mind and spirit.

PREDESTINATION

Predestination has always been a subject of theological debate. If God has predestined the course of human history, how can we be said to have free will? If our lives are predetermined in the mind of God, how can we be said to have any control over the outcome?

There can be three responses to this conundrum. The first suggests it's not worth worrying about; our fate has been sealed. In the words of the First World War song:

What's the use of worrying?
It never was worth while
So pack up your troubles in your old kit-bag,
And smile, smile, smile.

Remember, this jolly little ditty was sung by soldiers on their way to the Western Front, and so, with its exhortation to keep smiling the song reveals that rich vein of gallows humour typical of our music-hall tradition.

The second response is not to shrug and certainly not to smile, but instead to complain:

There once was a man who said, 'Damn!
It is borne in upon me I am
an engine that moves
in predestinate grooves,
I'm not even a bus, I'm a tram.

(Maurice Evan Hare 1889-1967)

The third response is that of the seventeenth century Norwich physician, Sir Thomas Browne. He stared with unflinching gaze at the question before declaring in magisterial prose that it was based on a false premise and was therefore not a problem at all. He wrote in his *Religio Medici:*

> *'Who can speak of Eternity without a solecism, or think thereof without an ecstasy? In eternity there is no distinction of tenses; and therefore that terrible term predestination, which hath troubled so many weak heads to conceive, and the wisest to explain, is in respect of God no prescious [foreknowing] determination of our estates to come, but a definitive blast of his will already fulfilled, and at the instant that he first decreed it; for to his eternity which is indivisible and all together, the last trump is already sounded, the reprobates in the flame and the blessed in Abraham's bosom.'*

So there we are. Simple really, isn't it? Quod erat demonstrandum.

RECTORY MICE

The Rectory has mice. It has always had mice. Ever since the present building was raised in the seventeenth century, generations of mice have enjoyed their freehold. From time to time the Rector of the day, or his wife, or his cook, or his gardener, or his cats, have tried, by fair means and foul, to evict the little beasts. To no avail. We are dealing here with a race of super-mice. We hear the patter of their feet as they scurry about behind the panelling, often at a level half-way up the wall. It worries the cats and drives the dogs mad. The noise of the younger set partying like crazy in the attic keeps us awake in the early hours.

Seldom do they appear. Rarely do they invade the kitchen – we make sure of that. Instead, they lead hidden lives in a parallel world to ours behind the wainscot, within the walls, beneath the floor, above the ceiling.

It is probable that within the seventeenth century structure of the present rectory there is concealed at least one former rectory, and possibly the one before that. In the fourteenth century the place was lived in by monks, the living of Withyham being a cell of the priory of Morteyn in Normandy. Inevitably, French mice concealed in the monks' baggage would have settled here and interbred with the indigenous population residing in Withyham rectory. As each building was constructed around its predecessor the mice remained, taking advantage of more spacious accommodation. Ours is not the only post-Reformation parsonage in England to be home to the descendants of pre-Reformation mice, proud of their recusant ancestry and Norman blood, and doubtless still loyal to the Bishop of Rome. For them King Henry's Act of

Supremacy and the Thirty Nine Articles were no more than transitory aberrations in the grand sweep of Catholic history.

These mice are part of that vast animal population, far more numerous than the human race, which shares with all of us this crowded world. They were on this planet before we came, and they will still be here after we have gone.

St Francis, as we all know, had a way with animals. But we seriously mistake him, if we see no more than a sweet little man in a friar's habit feeding the birds. Francis was tough as iron. He knew how nature worked. He fully understood that the survival of one living being depends upon the death of another, and that today's predator is tomorrow's prey. But he saw the glory of the Creator in creation, not least in the interdependence of all the species.

In one of the church's ancient canticles, the *Benedicite Omnia Opera*, we sing:

> *O all ye works of the Lord, bless ye Lord... O ye seas and floods... O ye whales and all that move in the waters... O all ye fowls of the air... O all ye beasts and cattle, bless ye the Lord, praise him and magnify him for ever.*

The list, with its implicit reference to sharks and jelly-fish, celebrates a world, not only glorious, but shot through with the harsh imperatives of survival.

SAINTS: ANCIENT & MODERN

A friend of mine recently gave me a book entitled *Saints and Sinners of the Marches*, compiled by Michael Tavinor, Dean of Hereford. It is a delightful volume, full of facts, quotations and pictures about the worthies and unworthies of Herefordshire and the Welsh Borders. The title does, however, beg the question: who is a saint and who is a sinner? Easy, you might say, Byron (yes, he's in there, having had a brief connection with Herefordshire) was a sinner, while, on the other hand, Woolos, the sixth century monk of Monmouth, who swam regularly and prayerfully in the freezing river with his wife Gwladys, and then ran about with no clothes on, was a saint – must have been, either that or mad.

But it is not so simple. Our perception of other people's goodness or sinfulness is bound to be inaccurate. Besides, our knowledge of ourselves as well as of others convinces us that it is part of the human condition that every man, woman, boy and girl is compounded of good and evil. For a Christian, only one human being has been perfect: Jesus Christ.

The original word 'saint' did not denote a person's goodness, but his or her discipleship. When St Paul uses the term 'saints' in his letters, he is referring to all the Christians gathered in one place; in Rome, say, or Corinth or Ephesus. They were all saints because they were all called to be followers of Christ, set apart by his grace. The goodness was Christ's, not theirs. You and I are saints by virtue of our being called to follow Our Lord, a vocation conferred by Baptism. How far we fall short of his perfection is manifestly evident to all.

However, the Church over the centuries adopted the convenient title 'Saint' to denote those who had made a singular contribution to the community of faith or to society at large. At first, the title was conferred informally and as a result of local initiative. In Saxon times every community liked to honour its own worthies, and nearly every local church had its own local saint complete with his or her own eccentric reputation (skinny-dipping while reciting the psalter or living in a cave or whatever).

Later, in the Middle Ages, the Church sought to tidy things up. Only those candidates for the title 'Saint' who had undergone a lengthy and searching process by the Roman Curia would be recognised as such. When the Church in England broke her links with Rome, becoming the Church *of* England, the former process of making a saint (canonisation) was no longer accessible to her. For four centuries no new names were added to the Anglican Calendar of Saints*, until recently when we have been adding new names without resorting to the cumbersome procedures still employed by Rome. In July, for example, we honour the memory of John Keble (July 14th) and William Wilberforce (July 30th). Saints or Sinners? Well, as always, neither, but a mixture of both.

---

* Except for Charles I, who was added to the BCP calendar of saints in 1662.

THOMAS BROWNE, PHYSICIAN

Physicians are inclined to take a pragmatic view of the human condition. They know too much about our bodies – and our minds – to be sentimental. They are realists. They know our limitations as patients, as surely as they know the limitations of medical science. After all, no cure is more than provisional. Sooner or later death gets us all.

Our picture of the family doctor is of someone with a sunny disposition. Not grim, not gloomy, not overcast by the dark clouds of mortality, but wise and comforting, even in the face of bad news. W H Auden put it like this:

> *Give me a doctor partridge-plump,*
> *Short in the leg and broad in the rump,*
> *An endomorph with gentle hands*
> *Who'll never make absurd demands*
> *That I abandon all my vices*
> *Nor pull a long face in a crisis,*
> *But with a twinkle in his eye*
> *Will tell me that I have to die.*

Thomas Browne, a GP of Norwich, lived in the seventeenth century at a time when medical science was emerging from the quackery of medieval superstition. His greatness lay not so much in his medical knowledge, which by later standards was very sketchy, but in his remarkable sanity and common sense in a century not known for either.

In his *Religio Medici* (A Physician's Religion) he wrote of the 'scandal of his profession'. He was referring to the commonly held view at that time that every doctor was a charlatan and an atheist, the assumption being that tinkering about with the human body was an interference with God's creation. 'And yet despite thereof,' wrote Browne, 'I dare, without usurpation, assume the style of Christian.'

In a century torn by fanaticism of one sort or another, Thomas Browne brought to the rancour of religious debate the healing touch of a physician's common sense. At a time when feelings about the conduct of worship ran so high that men came to blows over whether or not to kneel at prayer, or to make the sign of the cross at Baptism, he wrote, 'I am, I confess, naturally inclined to that which misguided zeal terms superstition. At my devotions I love to use the civility of my knee, my hat and hand.'

Put like that, who could quarrel with the sign of the cross; who could cavil at a genuflexion?

SLUMBERING ELEPHANTS

Our ancestors believed that elephants lacked joints in their legs, and so when these noble beasts wished to sleep, being unable to lie down, they would lean against the trees and gently nod off. From this our forebears concluded that the crafty bushman would saw halfway through the tree trunks, so that when the tired creatures reclined against them, the timber broke, precipitating them to the ground, where they would lie helpless, unable to rise again.

What is wrong with this ingeniously constructed scenario is not its absence of logic. It is, as you will agree, a supremely neat and logical account of how to hunt an elephant. What is wrong, however, is the premise upon which the argument rests. Given the false assumption that the elephant lacked joints, all else follows with faultless and compelling reason.

We are, on the whole, rational beings. We are for the most part reasonable and logical – certainly in our conscious attitudes. But below the sunlit slopes of rational thought, there lie in all of us those dark woods, seldom visited by the light of reason, where false assumptions gather like slumbering elephants beneath the trees.

One such assumption is that reality is objective; that the subjective world of our affections is less solid than the external world of things. So deeply felt is this assumption about the nature of reality that we use the word ' objective' to signify what is true and reliable, whilst we use the word 'subjective' to denote what is unreliable, partial, even distorted.

But what are we doing when we make this assumption? We are endorsing a view of reality which is quite contrary to that of the Bible and is ultimately ungodly and depressing. We are saying that the real world lies outside ourselves; outside those precious territories which are you and me, and beyond the boundaries of love, joy and hope. We are reducing reality to a harsh and sterile landscape where facts and figures lie impervious as boulders on the desert floor. And having stripped the scenery of its natural foliage of desire, we present this joyless waste as neutral reality, objective truth.

It is a chilling landscape we have made for ourselves. It is one dominated by those twin dragons: the laws of nature and the force of circumstance, leaving you and me ill equipped to survive in an alien land, with our vulnerable affections and unprotected hearts.

The Bible presents us with a picture of reality refreshingly different. One of the most powerful images it gives us is that of the Garden of Eden. Adam and Eve are in harmony with their environment and their maker. Reality is a garden in which trees and flowers, birds and beasts, man and woman, enjoy their creator as their creator enjoys them. All are caught up in that delight in living which pours like sunlight from the source of all being. It is a vision quite innocent of objectivity, for nothing in it, whether tree or flower, man or woman, rock or stream, stands outside the personal affection by which God embraces his world and by which his world embraces him.

But that is not the whole picture. If it were, it would be unhelpful to us as an image of reality. The picture also includes Adam and Eve's expulsion from the garden. Their exile into a horrible world where the personal relationship between creator and creation has been ruptured and replaced by the impersonal forces of existence; where mankind is alienated from his environment and his God. By this story we learn to recognise that our desire to reduce reality to the impersonal dimensions of facts and figures, and our morbid anxiety to drive that same reality out of the garden of divine affection into a wilderness of objectivity, is just another instance of our rebellion against our maker.

But even that is not the whole picture. There is another garden in the Bible. Just as the first Adam was raised by God from the ground to live in that earlier garden, so the second Adam, Jesus Christ, was raised that he might restore that garden to its creator. In that later garden, with the Risen Lord standing before the empty tomb, we see a token not only of redeemed humanity, but of a restored creation. Those physical fragments of Christ's earthly body, taken up, transformed and glorified by God in his risen body are signs to us that what we call the objective reality of the external world has been, is being, and will be, drawn back into the embrace of the creator's love. Signs that the substance of this world, its physical fabric, is ultimately the property of God.

Having before us, then, the evidence of Christ's resurrection, having within our hands the sacrament of his risen body how can we be blind to his risen glory in the world? Thomas Traherne, the seventeenth century mystic, wrote that if we but opened our eyes we should find the beams of earthly sunshine more delightful than the approach of angels, and the common air we breathe more precious than if it were crammed with crowns and sceptres.

The sun is but a little spark of God's infinite love; the sea but one drop of his goodness. But what flames of love ought that spark to kindle in our souls; what seas of affection ought to flow for that drop in our hearts. [*]

---

[*]   Thomas Traherne, Centuries of Meditations (ii: 7,12,14)

ST CUTHBERT'S, PHILBEACH GARDENS, 1949

To enter St Cuthbert's we had to push our way through heavy curtains which clung about our heads and threatened to suffocate. After a struggle we found ourselves inside a vast and gloomy basilica, whose lofty vault and gothic arches were shrouded in wafts of incense. My mother, whom I followed up the nave, seemed familiar with local custom and bobbed a genuflection towards the distant altar, then crossed herself as she knelt for a moment in private prayer. I did the same – that is to say, I crossed myself in the way I had learnt at my preparatory school where the headmaster's tractarian practice, learnt from his father, Athelstan Riley, encouraged a discreetly Catholic devotion: we crossed ourselves when grace was said in hall. I felt on this occasion a genuflexion was taking things too far.

As we sat and waited for the service to begin, I knew that I had experienced something like this once before. I remembered being once in the Church of the Holy Sepulchre, when we had lived in Jerusalem. Here again I was breathing the heavy scent of burning candles mingled with incense, and as I peered into the vault's deep shadows pierced by sudden shafts of light I could see again the glittering reflections on marble, silver, burnished copper and gold.

The service was High Mass, a mysterious and as yet unknown experience to a nine-year-old boy.

As the procession entered we could see crucifer and choir, thurifer with boat-boy, acolytes and servers in white albs, and finally the three sacred ministers of the Mass: priest, deacon and sub-deacon, gorgeously vested in chasuble, dalmatic and tunicle. So the great drama began.

I was held in thrall by the elaborate choreography with its chanting and its bells and its clouds of smoke. Among the robed figures upon that distant stage there glided to and fro as if on silent casters a plump acolyte. At intervals he struck a gong.

This was a more sacred experience than had been my encounter with Morning Prayer at another nearby church in Earl's Court. On that occasion the friendly vicar had meant well when after the service he had engaged me in some manly chat about the test match – England had just won the series against South Africa – but I shrank from his advances. At St Cuthbert's, Father Gage-Brown inhabited a different world. Aloof and austere, any such banter would have been, I felt, inappropriate, a dereliction, even, of his sacred office.

I had no idea what it all meant, this high ritual, nor did that matter. One thing was clear. Whatever was happening, it was of great importance. Here was solemnity needing neither explanation nor apology. It gave me sight of a world beyond the veil, a glimpse of heaven on earth; not that a nine-year-old would have articulated his feelings in those terms. The experience has never left me, nor been erased by a lifetime of worship in many different styles and many different places. I have never returned to St Cuthbert's in Philbeach Gardens nor to the Church of the Holy Sepulchre in Jerusalem, but what they gave me in my childhood seventy years ago is still part of me and will never be lost.

SUNDAY EVENSONG IN LATE SUMMER

O God, from whom all holy desires, all good counsels, and all just works do proceed: Give unto thy servants that peace which the world cannot give; that both our hearts may be set to obey thy commandments, and also that by thee we being defended from the fear of our enemies may pass our time in rest and quietness; through the merits of Jesus Christ our Saviour. Amen

(Book of Common Prayer:
The Second Collect of Evening Prayer)

Evensong on a late summer evening. We are lucky these days to have a choir to sing the office. After a hymn, the congregation settles to the rhythm of the Prayer Book. *'We have erred and strayed from thy ways like lost sheep. We have followed too much the devices and desires of our sinful hearts... we have left undone those things which we ought to have done, and we have done those things which we ought not to have done.'*

Later, the Second Collect reminds us that without God's grace our hearts are wayward, our deeds fall short: 'O God, from whom all holy desires, all good counsels, and all just works do proceed.' The prayer is ancient, its Latin origin earlier than the eighth century. Our medieval ancestors in their private devotions used the Middle English version: *'God, of whom ben hooli desiris, right councels and iust werkis...'* (fourteenth century Primer). Parson Richard Graye, my Tudor predecessor, would have been familiar with the Latin, *'Deus, a quo sancta desideria, recta consilia, et iusta sunt opera.'*, but like his generation of clergy he had to switch to the English of Cranmer's Prayer Book.

What of us this evening, as we make those words our own? Instinctively, we know that our desires this day have been less than holy and our intentions, though not entirely dishonourable, have not been pure. As for our works: have they been just? Well, perhaps – if you can dignify cooking lunch or mowing the lawn in such lofty terms.

However, that is just what St Benedict would have us do: sanctify the commonplace. The Prayer Book is redolent of his spirituality. And it is what George Herbert meant in his hymn we sang earlier:

Teach me, my God and King,
in all things thee to see;
and what I do in anything,
to do it as for thee.

'*Give unto thy servants that peace which the world cannot give.*' Jesus told his disciples on the eve of his arrest, '*Peace I leave with you, my peace I give unto you: not as the world giveth, give I unto you.*' The world's peace is a truce, a cessation. Christ's peace is different. He also said, '*I came not to send peace, but a sword.*'

Old Simeon knew about that sword when he told Mary that it would pierce her soul. We sing his words, '*Lord, now lettest thou thy servant depart in peace.*' In our small congregation this Sunday evening there is not a man or woman who has not felt that sword. May they be defended from the fear that kills. May they this evening find their rest and quietness in Christ.

SUNDAY SPORT

Now here's a tricky one. Just imagine that you are a parent with a child at foot, or two or three. You would like to bring them up as you yourself were brought up – and that includes going to church on Sunday. So you scout around until you find a church with a family service. At first, you feel a bit uncertain; it is so long since you went to church. Things are not the same as you remember. But after a few visits you begin to feel at home. The children get used to it too. They recognise some of their schoolmates. One of them joins the junior choir.

Then you find yourself – you're not sure why – on the coffee rota. Someone asks you if you or your other half would like to help at the church fête. Oh well, in for a penny, in for a pound. You begin to feel you belong. The Rector remembers your name. You even make sure that you stick that little yellow schedule of family services on the fridge door.

Then Sport kicks in. Ah yes, *Sport*. Sunday morning sport. Nothing wrong with team games on Sunday, but the consequences for the rest of the family can be dire. One son is asked to play for a local rugby team. Then, the other takes up cricket. Hardly a Sunday morning passes, winter or summer, without one or the other being called to play for his team. Would you stand in their way? Would you really? I know that I wouldn't. After all, when those children grow up, how will they regard a God, or a parent, who stopped them playing in a match and compelled them to let down their team?

Time passes and you find your Sundays unravelling. You become a taxi-driver for your children, sometimes for their friends as well. You become a peace-keeper, negotiating humiliating compromises with your non-sporty nine year old who sees no reason on earth why he or she should go to church when the others have a good time playing games. You try to 'hang in there' – after all, others seem to manage. So you keep trying. Then one terrible Sunday something inside you snaps. There you are struggling into church, late, wild-eyed, frazzled, dragging behind you a sullen child. You hear the opening hymn announced: *Give me joy in my heart, keep me praising.* 'Give me strength', you groan.

How lucky we grandparents were, when we were bringing up our children thirty years ago. In those uncomplicated days there were no team sports on Sunday morning. Sport was something that happened either on a weekday at school, or at the weekend on Saturday or on Sunday afternoon. Never a Sunday morning.

And so this is a message of affectionate sympathy to the present generation of young parents who do their best to bring up their children within the family of the church. We know it is so much more difficult for you than it was for us. This is also a message to any of you who give up your free time to coach future sportsmen and women: you are doing a great job for these youngsters, and for that we are all very grateful, but could you possibly, possibly avoid Sunday mornings?

THE ANGELUS AT WATERLOO

Midday and the train draws into London. A woman's recorded voice announces, 'The next station is Waterloo where this train terminates. Please remember to take all your personal belongings with you when you leave the train.' The man opposite speaks into his mobile phone, 'It's me. Running a bit late. Tell them to carry on without me. I'll be there as soon as I can.' I look at my watch and reckon there is time to say the Angelus.

The Angel of the Lord declared unto Mary
and she conceived by the Holy Ghost.

Three voices this noon caught into one instant of time: the woman's recorded announcement, the man's into his mobile, the angel's in Nazareth.

Hail, Mary, full of grace; the Lord is with thee.

Some months ago the owner of the recorded voice sat in a studio speaking her lines into a microphone. Who can tell how many thousands of commuters will hear those words repeated over and over again, until they merge with all the other background sounds of London's working day? And who among his fellow travellers can tell what decisions the businessman's colleagues might make in his absence? Meanwhile, the angel and Mary continue their dialogue:

Behold the handmaid of the Lord;
be it unto me according to thy word.

The voice of Mary uttering words of obedience and submission on behalf not only of herself, but of the entire human race. And that includes the passenger, late for his appointment, like a hundred others on this South West train, as they close their laptops with a sigh of irritation and gather up their papers.

Blessed art thou among women
and blessed is the fruit of thy womb, Jesus.

Another voice, this time Elizabeth's. She embraced her cousin, Mary, and completed the angel's greeting with her own words, *'Blessed art thou among women and blessed is the fruit of thy womb.'* Two expectant mothers caught up in God's plan to set us free, and each a slave to her own biological clock, one with nine months to wait and the other three. God, too, has to wait.

The Word was made flesh
and dwelt among us.

John the Evangelist wrote those words in the opening chapter of his gospel. Then, when he had written them, he recalled the amazing day when he, with Peter and James, saw Christ transfigured upon the mount. In parenthesis he added his personal testimony, *'And we beheld his glory, the glory as of the only begotten of the father, full of grace and truth.'*

John, an old man when he came to write down his memories and reflections, saw them against the backdrop of eternity. Luke, a young physician and a realist, described the Incarnation, that pivotal moment of our Redemption, as an event snared and trammelled by the contingencies of everyday life: the edict of Caesar Augustus, the government census, the legal requirement for Joseph to register at Bethlehem instead of Nazareth, the crowded inn, the shortage of accommodation, the stable, the unholy inconvenience of it all.

Pray for us, holy Mother of God,
that we might be made worthy of the promises of Christ.

And not just us, who know your story, who call you sister and try to follow your son, but pray for all those who never heard of him, or who having heard put his story aside as so much wishful thinking or so much nonsense. Pray for us, Mary, pray for us sinners, now at midday on Waterloo Station, and at the hour of our death when, sooner or later, our train makes its final stop and we must leave for ever our belongings, all our dear friends and those we love.

THE EIFFEL TOWER AND THE
SHADOW OF DEATH

In 1889 a French engineer of genius, Gustave Eiffel, constructed his remarkable tower. The people of Paris were slow to forgive him. Some never did. The writer, Guy de Maupassant, felt compelled to flee the city and finally to quit France altogether in order to escape what he called 'that unavoidable and tormenting nightmare.' Taking the contrary, but no less drastic action, the English designer and artist, William Morris, clambered into the tower and spent two weeks on the lowest platform, because only from there could he enjoy the views of Paris unspoilt by that 'ghastly and skeletal structure'.

Every so often in this world's history the human genius, without intending to do so, creates the shapes of its own nightmares. The Great Pyramid of Cheops, the Tomb of Mausoleus at Halicarnassus and the Tower of Babel were intended by their makers to defy mortality, but these massive works now share the fate of Shelley's Ozymandias. Of that great statue nothing remains but two vast and trunkless legs of stone and near them on the sand, half sunk, a shattered visage lies, while round the decay...

Of that colossal wreck, boundless and bare,
The lone and level sands stretch far away.

We would be fools to flee the unavoidable and tormenting nightmare of our own impending death. There are many escape routes which we might be tempted to take. We can surrender ourselves to pleasure, if we can afford the price, and if not, we can consume ourselves with envy. Or we can devote ourselves with unwholesome zeal to this season's good cause. And if we grow weary of improving others, we can apply ourselves to self-improvement, employ a style guru, become earnest about our diet and go for pointless runs in the morning mist.

But, unless terminally ill or in the grip of despair, we would be much greater fools deliberately to climb into death's embrace. A healthy awareness of the transience of this lovely world is no reason to despise its gifts. *'We brought nothing into this world, and it is certain that we can carry nothing out. The Lord gave and the Lord hath taken away; blessed be the name of the Lord.'* These words, familiar from the funeral service, remind us that though the Lord takes away, it is he who gives. This should give us an invincible delight in life's fragile beauty.

John Donne, the poet and Dean of St Paul's, used to keep his empty coffin in his bedroom. From time to time he would lie down in it to remind himself of his earthly destiny. You might think such behaviour grotesque. Yet his devotional verse and his sermons reveal not so much a sombre obsession with death, as a blazing and passionate belief in life. This prayer was fashioned by Dean Milner-White from one of Donne's sermons preached before the King at Whitehall:

> *Bring us, O Lord, at our last awakening into the house and gate of heaven, to enter into that gate and dwell in that house, where there shall be no darkness nor dazzling, but one equal light; no noise nor silence, but one equal music; no fears nor hopes, but one equal possession; no ends nor beginnings, but one equal eternity in the habitations of thy glory and dominion, world without end. Amen*

THE ETERNAL LITURGY AND
THE ONION SELLER

An Englishman, on holiday in Greece, decided to attend the Liturgy at the local village church. The small building was packed with a crowd of worshippers, who came and went as they pleased, lighting candles before the icons, crossing themselves and murmuring their private devotions.

Against this background of continuous disturbance the Liturgy unfolded its mystery, slowly, solemnly, magnificently.

Suddenly the Englishman felt someone pulling his sleeve. He turned to find a man holding a basket of onions. Would he like to buy some onions? No, no thank you. Why not? Was there anything wrong with the onions – perhaps they were bad onions? No, no they were excellent onions – but not now – perhaps after the Liturgy. 'After the Liturgy?' the Greek replied, '*After* the Liturgy? But the Liturgy…', and his look embraced the whole scene – the priest, the candles, the vestments, the incense, the music and the murmuring congregation, 'The Liturgy is *eternal.*'

At the Eucharist we hear the words which introduce us to the central mystery of worship – what the onion-seller understood as the eternity of the Liturgy:

Therefore with angels and archangels and all the company of heaven, we proclaim your great and glorious name, for ever praising you and saying, Holy, Holy, Holy Lord, God of power and might, heaven and earth are full of your glory. Hosanna in the highest.

The praise which we give, we did not initiate. The worship we offer, we did not begin. Before we enter church the cherubim and seraphim, those tremendous and eternal sentinels of heaven, are already singing Alleluias to their King. That is the sound which Isaiah heard when he saw '*the Lord, high and lifted up*' in the temple (Isaiah 6). John, too, heard it in his vision of heaven (Revelation 7). It has reverberated down the centuries in Jewish and, later, Christian worship in temple, synagogue, cathedral, church and chapel.

It began before the introit and it continues after we return home to prepare the vegetables, or read the papers, or wash the car.

We measure out our lives in tidy sequences. Breakfast, lunch, tea, supper. Today the golf course, tomorrow the office. Spring, summer, autumn, winter. Today a drive to Lewes, tomorrow the train to London Bridge.

But always beneath the surface noise of our daily lives, beneath the getting and the spending, the arrivals and departures, there lies that other continuum where the eternal liturgy unfolds its mystery, slowly, solemnly, magnificently.

THE LITTLE DOG LAUGHED

Hey, diddle diddle, the cat and the fiddle,
the cow jumped over the moon;
the little dog laughed to see such fun,
and the dish ran away with the spoon.

There he stands, that little dog, wagging his tail and barking with sheer joy. In his laughter there is no malice, no pin-prick of satire, no shadow of foreboding. You and I may wince at the cat's inexpert playing; see only folly in the cow's ecstatic leap ('she'll fall and break her leg. Then she'll be sorry'*);* shake our heads at the silly dish and spoon ('no good will come of it, mark my words'*).* But the little dog sees only fun, and laughs and laughs.

How innocent is our laughter? Much of what makes us laugh derives from other people's discomfort. We also laugh to ease our pain. We laugh too much, too long, too loud.

The TV's Gatling cackle of 'canned' studio laughter, overheard from another room, is a terrible noise. In it one hears the despairing sound of the human race crying from the abyss. *De profundis clamavi.* Perhaps the author of Ecclesiastes had this in mind when he said, '*As the crackling of thorns under a pot, so is the laughter of fools: this also is vanity.*'

Well, that's a pretty gloomy way of putting it. The fourth Earl of Chesterfield (1694–1773) had other reasons not to laugh. 'Having mentioned laughing,' he wrote to his son, 'I must particularly warn you against it… I am sure that since I have had the full use of my reason, nobody has ever heard me laugh.' He was against it. It was occasioned by low buffoonery. It made a nasty noise and distorted the features. It was ill-bred. Poor old Chesterfield.

In most of the instances of laughter in the Bible the cause is disbelief and scorn, not joy. Sarah laughed (Genesis, chapter 18) when she overheard the three angels telling Abraham that she, old Sarah, was going to have a baby. She was eavesdropping behind the tent door.

'Huh,' she snorted.

'You laughed?' they said.

'Who, me?'

'Yes, you.'

'I didn't laugh.'

'You did. You laughed.'

'What if I did?'

'You just wait,' they said, and left.

Nine months later she had good reason to laugh. This time for joy.

Unaffected laughter, untainted by malice or fear, is a rare and beautiful thing. Never is it more lovely than on the lips of captives set free:

> *When the Lord turned the captivity of Sion: then were we like unto them that dream.*
> *Then was our mouth filled with laughter: and our tongue with joy.*

> (psalm 126)

THE PITY OF WAR

We were in Normandy, staying in a cottage belonging to friends. Around us, as far as the eye could see, were lush pastures, little streams, apple orchards and the occasional half-timbered farmhouse. It was so beautiful. We could not have wished for more.

And yet that delightful and idyllic landscape was once, and not so long ago, torn up by war: its orchards uprooted, its houses burnt, its livestock lost, its people dispersed (many injured, and some killed) as sixty-four years ago the soldiers and the tanks of six nations – American, British, Canadian, French, German, Polish – slogged it out in the final battle to liberate Normandy. We were plum in the middle of what came to be known as the Falaise Gap. The little hill at nearby Montormel (a hamlet no bigger than Lye Green) was the pivot. It was the scene of unbelievable, suicidal, courage and terrible slaughter on all sides. Chiefly, it was the outnumbered Poles who bore the brunt and secured the victory.

Some of the older locals recall that for days afterwards a black cloud covered the landscape; this time it was not the smoke of shells, but a dense, vast, buzzing swarm of flies. For two months the stench was unbearable. Like Wellington after the Battle of Waterloo, General Eisenhower came to inspect the battlefield, and was sickened by what he saw. Amongst the bodies recovered was that of a young German soldier. He was thirteen years old.

Time passed. The orchards and crops grew again. The landscape recovered. Hostilities receded. Peace replaced and outlasted war. But not all injuries have been healed and not all rancour cured. Remembrance Sunday is an occasion to ponder these things.

War memorials, particularly those of the two World Wars of the twentieth century, are harsh reminders that it is the young and unknown, not the old and famous, who so often pay the highest price. But there are exceptions. In a small town in Northern France there is a memorial to those who fell at the nearby Battle of Crécy in 1346. Among them was King John of Bohemia. He was killed, as were a large number of the French nobility, under a hail of arrows from the English longbows. He was an old man, and he was blind. He had ridden into battle, with his charger roped to the horses of two knights who rode on either side.

Shakespeare's Othello, that great commander, spoke nostalgically of war:

> *Farewell the neighing steed and the shrill trump,*
> *The spirit-stirring drum, the ear-piercing fife,*
> *The royal banner, and all quality,*
> *Pride, pomp and circumstance of glorious war.*

But at what cost? A thirteen-year-old boy dead? A blind, old king unhorsed and killed? Another poet, Wilfred Owen, awarded the MC for courage and killed on the Western Front a week before the armistice in 1918, put the matter more starkly when he wrote about 'The pity of war'. The heart-wrenching, mind-searing pity.

THE QUEEN'S DIAMOND JUBILEE

Where were you on Wednesday 6th February 1952 at 11.15 am? That was the moment when the BBC announced the death of King George VI. It was also the moment when Princess Elizabeth became Queen – such is the unbroken continuity of the British Constitution. Where were you at that moment – if indeed you were alive sixty-five years ago. I remember exactly where I was. I was sitting in a classroom with about twenty other bored teenagers listening to a remarkably patient teacher as he explained the second law of thermodynamics. The subject was designated 'Science for non-scientists', which was a give-away. Not only were we non-scientists, we were 'non' almost everything else. We were all fourteen years old. The worst age.

Halfway through his discourse the master was interrupted by the arrival of a prefect bearing a written message. He read it, paused and then said, 'Gentlemen, the lesson is suspended. The King has died. Please stand.' The awe and solemnity were palpable; so palpable that even callow youth sensed the shock.

Inevitably, a Royal Jubilee is the anniversary of a departure as well as an arrival: 'The King is dead, Long live the King' (or, in this case, 'the Queen'). Also inevitably, and understandably, it is the Queen's accession and not her father's death we commemorate. However, during those bleak February days sixty-five years ago the sombre mood of a nation mourning her King had to be experienced before we could move on to enjoy the coronation of his daughter. Added to the burden of her unexpected accession, she herself had to endure the loss of a beloved father, and to do so in the glare of one of the most public offices on earth.

What happened to those twenty 'non scientists'? Well, they grew up, some to become lawyers, some accountants, some broadcasters, some pastors and teachers. One became a composer, one a circuit judge, and one, possibly the gentlest and most civilised of us all, a member of MI6. Having left school, our paths rarely crossed. New patterns of friendship replaced the old. I do wonder, however, whether the Queen's Diamond Jubilee triggered in their minds faint memories of the classroom where they were and the people they were with on that Wednesday morning when the new reign began.

A nation needs shared symbols and events by which to construct and celebrate her nationhood. You can rattle off a list easily enough: Big Ben, the Union Jack, the Cenotaph, Wimbledon, Blackpool Tower, Ascot, the Cup Final, the Promenade Concerts... and so on. Our country is lucky in having as its most potent symbol the Queen. Not only is she a focus for the United Kingdom, but over the past sixty-five years she has created a vast network of shared memories in the minds of millions of her subjects, of whom those twenty 'non-scientists' are just a tiny part.

THE TWILIGHT OF DUBIETY

You may be one of those happy people who know their own mind. Someone who, whatever the issue, can always be relied upon to have an opinion; what's more, an opinion firmly held, clearly stated, oft repeated. Unknown to you are the shadows of doubt. Charles Lamb, the essayist, described such a person thus: 'The twilight of dubiety never falls upon him. Is he orthodox? He has no doubts. Is he an infidel? He has none either. Between the affirmative and the negative there is no border-land with him.'

Now, if you do enjoy the daylight of continuous certainty, then you are indeed happy. You are also a great nuisance, and almost certainly wrong. The danger of knowing your own mind is that you may come to know little else.

Of course, there are certain experiences in life which evoke an immediate response. It need not take you long to make up your mind about the Albert Memorial – your response will be either 'Yea' or 'Nay'. Nor would you wish to suspend judgement indefinitely over the Bactrian camel. To affect impartiality would be absurdly pedantic.

But there are many matters about which we can never be so certain. We inhabit a region of doubt, a border-land set between two zones of certainty. On the one hand there is the region inhabited by animals and new born babes: it is the present moment, where things are what they are. On the other hand, there is the region inhabited by the angels: eternity, where there is no shadow of turning and things will be what they will be. But between these two states of innocence, is ours: a twilight zone where things are not what they should be, and could be what they aren't.

Dogs recumbent in the sun, little children and mad old saints in caves are able to inhabit the present moment. They respond directly to experience. You and I, who have lost our innocence, are banished from the holy present which is also the Holy Presence. As exiles we can only catch glimpses of that Presence through the veil of our own self-awareness. Experience of beauty and encounters with the divine are momentary. As soon as they happen, our busy minds take over and our encounter with the present is in the past. Moses and the Burning Bush, the disciples at the Transfiguration, Saul on the road to Damascus – those burning flashes of blinding light which they experienced were just that: momentary glimpses, yielding to a lifetime's reflection. We, like they, are condemned to spend our lives inside our conscious minds at one remove from reality.

Now, because we cannot bear too much beauty, we talk about it instead. Too sinful to endure the burning presence of God, we talk about him instead. Theology, like musical criticism, belongs to our fallen nature. In heaven we will be too busy singing to read the reviews. And, should we chance to bump into St Thomas Aquinas, and have the cheek to ask him about his massive *Summa Theologica*, he will almost certainly answer with a shrug, 'Straw, just so much straw.'

You and I may be given during our lifetime once, twice, three times perhaps, such an experience of certainty. When that happens, we will share momentarily with the animals, the saints and the angels their immediate response to the Creator; we will step briefly into the present moment where things are as they are and God is as he is. In that moment we will see enough reality to sustain us through the years of uncertainty until he brings us into the eternal present which is his eternal presence.

BETWEEN IDEA AND REALITY
FALLS THE SHADOW

Thomas Sheraton died, as he had lived, in poverty. And yet in his lifetime and for a couple of decades after his death, his was one of the defining influences on English furniture design. Next time you watch a film or TV production set in the eighteenth century look at the elegance of the chairs and tables, and you will probably be looking at designs inspired by Sheraton.

When someone called upon him at his workshop, which was also his home, in Soho, the visitor was shocked by the squalor. He sat on a broken chair. There was filth on the floor. When tea was offered, there were only two cups and Mrs Sheraton had to surrender hers to the guest and drink from a bowl. Yet it was here that designs were drawn for England's most graceful and pleasing furniture.

'Between the idea and the reality falls the shadow'. There is nothing new about this huge disparity between the artist and his art. Edward Gibbon, composer of some of the most fastidious English prose, was afflicted by a sickness which made him gross and, at times, very smelly. Dr Johnson, arbiter of morals and sound common sense, ate with his mouth open and spilt his food down his coat.

I suppose that we should not allow the reality to diminish the art. But it is hard not to let the shortcomings of the artist's life, both involuntary and otherwise, influence our appreciation of his work.

We are all caught in the shadow between idea and reality. Turning to ourselves as both artist and work of art, we know what we are, and we know what we should be. We know what we do, and we know what we should do. As St Paul wrote – and you can hear the desperation in his voice – 'The good that I would, I do not: but the evil which I would not, that I do.'

The good news is this: ultimately we are in the hands of a greater artist than ourselves, a master-craftsman who will take our lives and re-create them. Between his idea of what we truly can be and the reality of what we truly will be, there will be no shadow of separation. And that is what we mean by Heaven.

But we still have a long way to go!

UNRULY WILLS AND AFFECTIONS

It is believed by some that an important factor in the blood-soaked annals of Scottish history was the interminable Caledonian winter. For month after month the clansmen would endure imprisonment within their dank granite walls, with nothing to do but glower at their wives and think murderous thoughts about mankind.

Come the 1st of May and the first hint of summer, they would rush outdoors, claymore in hand, and fall upon their nearest neighbours.

Meanwhile, our ancestors south of the border celebrated May Day in different fashion. They put flowers in their hair, sang 'hey-nonny-nonny-no', and were jocund on the village green.

If our temperament is captive to our climate, how much more beholden is it to the caprice of fortune and the accident of adversity. Edith Sitwell, in her mission to tease the philistines, was impelled by a deep distrust of the drab and the boring. This aversion had been formed at an early age, when she first began to feel the menace of an unsympathetic world. Of her nursery-maid, Martha, the five year old Edith was heard to complain in tones of shrill exasperation, 'She does nothing to amuse me and everything to displease me.' By such seemingly trivial provocations the adult temperament is formed.

But it is not only the accident of past adversity which shapes our temperament (our unruly affections); we are also the playthings of our present moods. Beneath the bland surface of our lives there run conflicting currents of passion, envy, lust, malice, vaulting ambition and pious aspiration. We are Heathcliff, Othello, Tamburlaine the Great, Teresa of Lisieux and Lady Macbeth. At times we are St Francis; at times Attila the Hun. No wonder we find it hard to behave.

Some of our unruly affections are glaringly corrupt. The temptation to be Lady Macbeth or Attila the Hun is one which is probably best resisted. Less obvious, perhaps, is the need to fight the temptation to be St Francis of Assisi or St Teresa of Lisieux. Aspiration to sanctity is the first step to spiritual ruin.

What then are we to do? If all our affections are corrupt – if even our kindly instincts are suspect, what on earth *can* we do? Well, we can start by looking again at the Collect for the fourth Sunday after Easter (in *Common Worship* it is allocated to the third Sunday before Lent):

> *O Almighty God, who alone canst order the unruly wills and affections of sinful men: Grant unto thy people, that they may love the thing which thou commandest, and desire that which thou dost promise; that so among the sundry and manifold changes of this world, our hearts may surely there be fixed where true joys are to be found.*

God alone can control our turbulent desires. He alone can order our unruly affections. But we must let him enter our private kingdoms. If we but allow him to gain a foothold, he will extend his dominion bit by bit across the territory of our souls, liberating us from our adversaries within. He will capture our affections, one by one; not only those shameful ones we keep hidden from view, but also those honourable ones upon which we strive to build our public reputations. His tactics may be unpredictable, his strategy obscure, but our faith is this: that his purpose is irresistible. He will master us in the end, for his is the kingdom, the power and the glory, for ever and ever.

WEDDINGS

It is the season for weddings; a good time, therefore, to examine what exactly it is we mean by a 'church wedding'.

When I took my first weddings in Coventry fifty years ago, the meaning was clear. The couple, usually in their early twenties, sometimes in their teens, would come to church for a ceremony which would allow them to enter a new (and in most cases untried) relationship. The pews were filled with parents, uncles, aunts, grandparents and friends of the parents, who spent the service staring with deep suspicion at their opposite numbers across the aisle. There was a palpable uneasiness about many of those weddings.

How things have changed for the better! A wedding today is not usually the creation of a new union, but the consecration of an existing one. And surely that must be a good thing. At least the couple know what they are in for. As an officiating priest, I know that weddings are nowadays far more relaxed, and for that reason far happier occasions than ever they used to be.

An older generation might regret this state of affairs. However, the situation is not new. Until comparatively recently, and certainly until the mid-eighteenth century when Parliament sought to regulate marriage (and did this not on moral grounds, but to protect the property of the landed classes from the consequences of their children's rash liaisons) it was regarded as a private compact which could be entered into before witnesses, and not necessarily in church. The law recognised the validity of such marriages.

From this it can be seen that what made the marriage was the consent declared by the couple to each other before witnesses. However desirable the church's blessing may have been in terms of pastoral discipline, according to canon law a religious ceremony was not necessary to effect or validate the union. Understandably the clergy often taught differently, but they did so against the teaching of their own canonists

It was accepted that a couple might be betrothed by means of a contract, undertaken perhaps in the parental home, months, sometime years, before being solemnised in church. The word used was 'Solemnise', suggesting that the church's role was not to create, but to dignify an existing relationship. In medieval law, especially when inheritance was an issue, the rights of children born before the church ceremony had taken place were not in jeopardy. The concept of wedlock was far wider than our modern attitudes allow. It was seen to be a status which the couple could legitimately confer upon themselves, and not one created by permission of church or state. The Marriage Act of 1753 and succeeding legislation changed all that.

An earlier Royal Marriage – that between King Richard II and Anne of Bohemia in 1382 – was celebrated by Chaucer in his allegory, 'Parliament of Fowls'. In this poem God's deputy who presides over love and marriage is not the Church, which is what you might expect in an age when the clergy sought to control every aspect of life. It was 'the goddess Nature'. By the strange convolutions of history the church's role today at a wedding, which is, in practice at least, to bless an existing relationship, rather than to confer a new one, is now closer to its origins than it has been for centuries.

WHAT'S IN A NAME?

Driving through Normandy on our summer holiday I came across a statue erected to the sacred memory of St Opportune. St *who*? You may well ask. I had to look her up. She was the sister of St Chrodegang and cousin to St Lantildis. Sanctity ran in their family, though not so strongly as one might have hoped. Another cousin, Chrodobert, envious of Chrodegang's episcopal possessions, hired an assassin to kill the bishop. Those were the bad old days of Merovingian France, when dragons stalked the land, and kings and saints had names like Chilperic, Dagobert and Clothilde.

But *Opportune*? She led a cloistered and blameless life, founded a convent, and became its abbess. It is her name, however, which stands out. It does not sound Frankish. It does not sound plausible. What, one wonders, were the child's parents thinking of when, in answer to the priest's request at her christening to 'name this child', they said, 'Opportune'? Was it a statement of gratitude for a timely birth, or a pious hope for the child's future?

History is full of examples of names which have been chosen, not so much as the child's label of identity, but as an expression of the parents' current preoccupations. Ichabod – a Biblical name meaning 'the glory has departed' – was used at royalist christenings following the execution of Charles I in 1649, and, eleven years later, at parliamentarian ones to lament the collapse of the Commonwealth. In 1834, at a time when the Church of England was in grave trouble, Mr and Mrs Bennett of Faversham named their little boy Thomas Churchreform Bennett.

It was once not uncommon for parents, moved by an

aspiration more pious than prudent, to name their daughters Chastity, and their sons Endeavour. Heartfelt gratitude underlay the naming of Dorothy and Theodore (both the same name – Dora Thea or Theo Dorus – meaning 'Gift from God'). Mr and Mrs Frewen's joy at the birth of their son, however, seems to have been less than jubilant when they named him Accepted. This lack of parental enthusiasm did not prevent his becoming, in 1644, the Archbishop of York.

What, one wonders, could the grandparents of Arthur Onslow, Speaker of the House of Commons in the eighteenth century, have been thinking of when they named their son *Foot?* Was it a mistake arising from the parson being deaf... or the godfather being drunk? A lifetime of jokes about his name did not inhibit his rise through the civil service to become First Commissioner of Excise in the service of King George II.

There is good Biblical precedence for using names to make a statement. The most famous being the divine command conveyed by the angel Gabriel that the Son of God be called *Jesus* (Saviour). Our Lord himself nick-named Simon 'Peter' (the Rock), and the irascible brothers James and John he called *Boanerges* (Sons of Thunder).

We receive our names from our parents, and our nick-names from our friends; to that extent we carry with us through our lives the hopes and opinions of others. We do not name ourselves, and have no right to do so. At our most personal level we belong not to ourselves, but to others, and ultimately by our christening we belong to Christ.

WHERE IS PLANTAGENET?

'Time hath his revolutions; there must be a period and end to all things temporal, an end of names and dignities... For where is Bohun? Where is Mowbray? Where is Mortimer? Nay, which is more and most of all, where is Plantagenet? They are entombed in the urns and sepulchres of mortality.'

Thus spoke Lord Chief Justice Ranulph Crewe in his judgement in the Oxford Peerage Case (1625); a reminder to our generation that nostalgia for the past is nothing new. Even in the age of Ben Jonson and at a time when Shakespeare still lived in people's memory, there was a yearning for the glory of a more distant past. They did not speak of Raleigh, Frobisher or Drake, the heroes of the Elizabethan past, but of Bohun, Mowbray, Mortimer and, 'which is more and most of all', Plantagenet. That great roll-call of fabled names still had the power to move the Court of King's Bench in its dustiest and driest deliberations.

'Where' – we might cry today, but with less elegance of diction – 'Where is Quinquagesima? Where is Sexagesima? Nay, which is more and most of all, where is Septuagesima? They are consigned to the attic of discarded and forgotten texts'.

Septuagesima and her two younger sisters are the names our ancestors gave to the three Sundays we now know by their numerical position before Lent: the Third Sunday before Lent, the Second Sunday before Lent and the Sunday Next Before Lent.

As children we would marvel in the school chapel at the three 'Gesimas' – such sonorous names. Mysterious, polysyllabic, and gloriously unintelligible, like that line at the end of a favourite hymn, 'Consubstantial, co-eternal, while unending ages run'. How rich and resonant was the language of worship, how arcane, and how full of surprises when later we learnt its meaning.

As pupils, we came upon this discovery by chance, by a pleasing serendipity. 'Turn to your Latin grammars,' said the headmaster, 'page 46. Revise your numerals up to a hundred.' *Unus, duo, tres, quattuor...* My eyes wandered to the parallel column – *primus, secundus, tertius, quartus*. And on and on down the column, down to the magnificent multisyllabic *centensimus vicensimus sextus* (126th). And there they were, those three mysterious figures, exotic as the Magi: *Septuagesima, Sexagesima, Quinquagesima* (seventieth, sixtieth, fiftieth).

The penny dropped. What could be more plain? The seventieth day before Easter, the sixtieth and the fiftieth. True, the arithmetic was faulty, but we took that to be a minor deviation. You could hardly call the third Sunday before Lent the sixty-third day before Easter. Far too pedantic. Besides, had we not learnt that the French called a fortnight *une quinzaine*? One need not be too exact in such matters.

But now we have lost our Septuagesima and her two sisters. Ah well, 'Time hath his revolutions; there must be… an end of names and dignities'. A shame, but there we are. There is some consolation though. Our revised church calendar is not without its pleasing quirks. It has given us the sparkling crackle of 'Pentecost' to replace the familiar 'Whitsun', which means that we now have a Greek word for a Hebrew festival in place of an English word for a Christian festival. Liturgy must have her little jokes, else how po-faced she would be. Not only that. Without these small clues to her ancient roots how impoverished she would become.

WORDS, WORDS, WORDS

'Words, words, words,' said Hamlet teasingly to Polonius. And then, many hundreds of words later, the tormented, dying prince spoke his last sentence 'The rest is silence.' We utter so many words during our life's span before that final silence.

Where do they go, all those little words? I was once told – it seemed an implausible theory, but it has haunted me ever since – that the sound of every syllable, once uttered, reverberates for ever and ever, fainter and fainter, a diminishing, but never ending oscillation of the sound waves, needing only a super-sensitive receiver, a cat's whisker, to pick it up. Just think: not only our honourable words orbiting for ever, but our less gracious utterances too: the lies, the jeers, the insults; all the din of our fallen humanity.

There are two stories in the bible about words. One tells of their power to confuse: the other their power to unite. When men built the Tower of Babel (Genesis 11) they said '*Go to, let us build us a city and a tower, whose top may reach unto heaven; and let us make us a name.*' But God punished their arrogance. He confused their language. Where there had been a single tongue, now there were many. The work came to a stop. The tower fell into ruin. Babel undone by babble.

The second story mirrors the first, but the image is reversed. When on the day of Pentecost (Whitsun) God's Holy Spirit came down upon the disciples in tongues of fire and with a rushing mighty wind (Acts 2), those unlettered Galileans were empowered to communicate their faith to foreigners despite the language barrier. The crowd, drawn from every nation known to the writer, exclaimed in amazement, '*We do hear them speak in our own tongues the wonderful works of God.*' The unifying

Word of God miraculously overcame the diversity and the babble of human language.

The Word of God, made flesh in Christ and diffused throughout creation by his Holy Spirit, reconciles, heals, and draws the poison of our guilt. On the Cross the Word is the victim of our malicious words, the lies, the jeers, the insults. In every friend or enemy at whom we ever aimed a sly malicious dart Christ is the target. '*Inasmuch as ye have done it unto one of the least of these my brethren, ye have done it unto me.*' Those nasty little words that for ever echo in our memory, words which we can never unsay – though how we wish we could – are felt by him, and then, if we allow it, their reverberation is stilled at last by his forgiving love. And those whom we have hurt – what if there is no opportunity to say sorry, or what if they cannot forgive us? Well, that is our penance. Our words carry within them their own reward.

COURTESY

(From a sermon preached in Guildford Cathedral at the Sung Eucharist on Trinity 5, 1987)

> *'Be ye all of one mind, having compassion one of another, love as brethren, be pitiful, be courteous.'*
>
> (Peter 3:8)

We are told by St Peter that we should be courteous. And courtesy is a quality so sweet, gracious and amiable, that surely it must need no deliberate cultivation. And yet experience teaches us otherwise

Courtesy is like the flowers around us this morning. It needs cultivation. Now, you might think that courtesy has to do with the artificial manners of the court, and, as such, is unsuitable to the followers of Jesus Christ. You may believe that the rustic simplicity of the peasant is closer to God's heart than the contrived manners of the courtier.

But the word 'courtesy' has an earlier meaning. By one of those instructive coincidences of language, it comes from the same Latin stem as the word for garden. *'Hortus'*, and its derivative *'cohors'*, meaning a small cultivated enclosure, have given us two related words. *Hortus* gives us 'horticulture', and *cohors* gives us 'court' and hence the manners of the court.

Ever since God planted a garden East of Eden and placed in it Adam and Eve to tend it, mankind has had to work hard to acquire the twin skills of gardening and good manners.

Now, there arises the question of sincerity. How Christian is it to cultivate good manners, if the effect is to conceal murderous thoughts? Is it right that you and I should present to the world a well-ordered, tidy, gracious conversation, and keep hidden from view the wild and lawless countryside within?

We are faced with a dilemma. Either we are polite and hide our true feelings, and are dissemblers, or we say exactly what we think, and are discourteous.

Capability Brown had the answer – or, rather, his predecessor and mentor, William Kent. It was Kent's ideas on garden design which helped to create much of the English landscape. His notion was to break down the barrier between the formal garden and the uncultivated countryside which lay outside. Hitherto the fashion had been to create a highly artificial enclosure of gravelled walks, clipped hedges and rectangular basins, and to shut out the world of untamed nature. William Kent changed all that. He designed his gardens so that there was continuity between art and nature. He replaced the rigid geometry of the formal garden with a gentler style, where the shrubs and trees were gathered in informal groups, where water was taught to meander seemingly at its own pleasure, and where the natural contours of the distant scene were drawn into the foreground design.

The garden wall was taken down and nature was invited in (although a judiciously placed ha-ha kept the cattle out). In the words of Horace Walpole, William Kent had 'leaped the fence, and saw all nature was a garden.'

Courtesy – true courtesy – is found at the place where the two worlds connect. Now, you and I, because we are sinners, can find only a very narrow margin where artifice and nature touch and overlap. Courtesy, as we practise it, is more often a pretence. But it is our hope that by God's grace, through the power of Christ's redeeming love, we will be so converted that looking into our hearts we shall find there, no longer a rough countryside, but we shall see within the enclosure of our souls that all nature is a garden.

FRIENDS

(From a sermon preached at Holy Trinity Church, Guildford, on Rogation Sunday 2000)

'You are my friends if you do what I command you.
I do not call you servants any longer, because the
servant does not know what the master is doing,
but I have called you friends because I have made
known to you everything that I have heard from the Father.'

(John 15:9–17)

Jesus calls us his friends. No longer mere servants in the kingdom of God, we are to be more than that. He calls us to a higher status: we are to be his friends.

The notion of Friendship does not often occur in the language of religion. Love occurs frequently. Love carries theological weight. God loves us, and we aspire to love him. In this context 'Love' is a religious word.

'Fellowship' is another religious word. We talk about the fellowship of the Eucharist and the fellowship of the Church. The Greeks had a word for it: *'koinonia'*. But the word has moved away from its plain secular roots, and has acquired cloyingly pious overtones. We might, for example, say as we stack the plates in the dishwasher after a successful dinner party, 'my goodness, that was a great evening – *how richly blessed we were in our fellowship'* – or, at least, I don't suppose you would say it unless with heavily ironic emphasis and simpering expression.

'Fellowship' is a word no longer easily employed in ordinary conversation. It carries the moist imprint of religion's clammy hand.

But 'Friendship': now, there's a word that remains stubbornly secular. Unpretentious. Clean. Straightforward. Honest. Free of all sanctimosity. It denotes the voluntary bond of affection joining equal to equal with the softest and gentlest cords.

On the whole, religion cannot accommodate friendship as easily as it can discipleship, servanthood or fellowship – all of which bring to mind elements of discomfort and strain. Friendship, on the other hand, is easy and relaxed. It requires no effort or dissimulation. It can be unpredictable, even wild and anarchic. It has a wide and sometimes unexpected configuration, bringing us into strange, even disreputable, company. It does not fit piety's tight frame.

The haphazard cords which bind us to our friends intersect so many other lines of loyalty, cross so many boundaries of age, place, religion and culture. The connections they make stretch far beyond the limits of our religion.

Jesus said '*You are my friends if you keep my commandments*' – no longer servants, but friends – he liberates us from the bonds of religion. But he does something else too.

By using the secular language of friendship he opens a door into those rooms in our lives where people come and go, laughing, chatting, whispering, crying, singing – all those people whom we hold dear; all those people we love and all those who love us.

Christ opens the door, slips quietly in and joins the party.